√3

Dual Ring Dog

The ultimate dual ring dog in the opinion of many is the celebrated Doberman Pinscher, Ch. Royal Tudor's Wild As the Wind, CDX, owned by Art and Sue Korp and Beth Wilhite. "Indy" established a number of impressive show ring records for Dobermans and for all Working breeds. She was Best in Show at the 1989 Westminster Kennel Club show under Mrs. Bernard Freeman, and in the same year, Best of Breed at the largest Specialty of the Doberman Pinscher Club of America held to that time. She is shown here in that win under the premier breed authority, Peggy Adamson, and handled by Mrs. Korp. *Mikron*

Dual Ring Dog

Jacqueline Fraser
and
Amy Ammen

Training Photos by Jan Plagenz
Cartoons by Geoffrey A. Ellis

HOWELL
BOOK HOUSE

New York

Maxwell Macmillan Canada
Toronto

Maxwell Macmillan International
New York   Oxford   Singapore   Sydney

Howell Book House
Macmillan Publishing Company
866 Third Avenue
New York, NY 10022

Maxwell Macmillan Canada, Inc.
1200 Eglinton Avenue East, Suite 200
Don Mills, Ontario M3C 3N1

Macmillan Publishing Company is part of the Maxwell Communication Group of Companies.

Library of Congress Cataloging-in-Publication Data
Ammen, Amy.
    Dual ring dog / Amy Ammen and Jacqueline Fraser ; training
photo by Jan Plagenz : cartoons by Geoffrey A. Ellis.
        p.   cm.
    ISBN 0-87605-539-0
    1. Dog—Showing.   2. Dogs—Obedience trials.   3. Dogs—Training.
I. Fraser, Jacqueline.   II. Title.
SF425.A7   1991
636.7'088'8—dc20   91-29068   CIP

Macmillan books are available at special discounts for bulk purchases for sales promotions, premiums, fund-raising, or educational use. For details, contact:

Special Sales Director
Macmillan Publishing Company
866 Third Avenue
New York, NY 10022

10 9 8 7 6 5 4 3

Printed in the United States of America

To my Parents: David and Dori Freedman
JF

To my Students: Friends and teachers
AA

Contents

NOVICE: Earning the Green

NOVICE: Turning It Blue

OPEN: Earning the Green

OPEN: Turning It Blue

UTILITY: Earning the Green

UTILITY: Turning It Blue

The American Staffordshire Terrier, Ch. Kirkee's Polar Bear O' Fraja, EC, CD, co-owned and trained by Jacqueline Fraser, is truly a dual ring dog. She is shown in an important conformation victory—Best of Breed at the Staffordshire Terrier Club of America Specialty under judge Florise M. Hogan, Ms. Fraser handling. *David Skeeters*

Chew On This

All breeds of dogs are capable of performing the obedience exercises. No training problem is unique to any breed.

Introduction

AMY AND I don't agree on much.

Amy trains her dogs slowly and thoroughly, moving from one step to another only after the first step has been perfected and proofed. Always in a hurry, I move from one step to the next as soon as my dog does the first step well enough to get a passing score most of the time.

When Amy decides her dog is ready for competition, it will compete for a long time. She trains her dogs all the way through Utility before entering them in Novice. Once entered, they show until they have all their titles and then continue competing for awards and points toward an obedience trial championship (OTCh.). When I think my dog has a decent chance of passing, I show her until she earns her title. Then I stop entering her in obedience until she is trained for the next title. In between she may be specialed or bred while I start another dog in obedience.

Amy believes that when teamed with a good trainer-handler, an average dog of any breed is capable of earning a Utility Dog title, class placements and even an OTCh. Her pet peeve is trainers who underestimate a dog's competitive potential because of breed. I am one of those trainers. I make allowances for terriers because they were bred to be alert to their surroundings and thus are easily distracted. I make allowances for toys because long grass, hair on the mat and uneven ground are obstacles to a tiny dog. But I don't discriminate. If allowances are needed, I will make them for a Golden Retriever.

When Amy enters the obedience ring, she hopes to leave with two ribbons.

Ideally, one of them will be blue. When I enter the obedience ring, my mission is accomplished if I leave with a green qualifying ribbon.

Amy uses the breed ring to show that her high-scoring obedience dogs are good, sound representatives of their breed. I use the obedience ring to prove that my champion brood stock is intelligent and trainable.

Our differences are physical and mental as well as philosophical. Amy performs with the self-confidence of a natural. I fight a never-ending battle against stage fright.

When Amy was eleven years old, she bought a Husky named Tess and trained her to an American and Canadian UD. Born graceful and aided by an early start, Amy learned, then modified and perfected, a winning style based on smooth footwork and subtle head cues. When I attended my first obedience class, I was older than Amy is now. Years of childhood dancing lessons failed to make me graceful. After fifteen years in obedience rings, it still feels as if little gremlins are skipping around my feet, laughing mischievously as they make me step on my own toes and trip over my dog. Finally, I can make use of them. Since I know these gremlins well, I'll warn you with them when we get to their favorite exercises.

With so many differences, how did Amy and I manage to write this book? Well, we agree on important things. Both of us believe when dogs compete in obedience *and* conformation they have an advantage in both rings. Both of us want our dogs to reach their highest potential. That Amy's reach theirs in the obedience ring while mine find glory in the breed ring really doesn't matter. Both of us have proven that breed dogs are intelligent and are not confused by obedience training and that obedience-trained dogs are more confident and responsive in the breed ring.

As you read our book, think of Amy as an obedience major with a minor in conformation and me as a breed ring major with a minor in obedience.

Each obedience exercise is going to appear in two sections. My portion, ''Earning the Green,'' will tell you what your dog must already know before proceeding to each new exercise and what actually is new about the exercise. It will break the lesson into manageable parts, bring the parts together and explain how some exercises tie in with conformation. After detailing the responsibilities and common errors in dogs and handlers, I'll let you know what mistakes you can get away with and still pass. Amy's section, ''Turning it Blue,'' will help you shape winning performances by adding fine points, like polished competitive

---

Because this book was conceived with the breeder in mind, and most breeders keep more bitches than males, the majority of dual-ring dogs will be female. To honor our delightful dual-ring dams, and yours, we broke tradition and referred to the dog throughout this book as "she" rather than "he."

footwork and subtle head cues. She discusses teaching aids to enhance motivation and speed and lets you in on how she prevents boredom while practicing for perfection.

Thank you for reading our book. Whether you choose to settle for the green or strive for the blue, we hope our methods will help you enjoy your dogs while accomplishing your goals.

Jacqueline Fraser

The Bullmastiff, Ch. Blackslate's Megan Force, CD, owned by Bonnie J. Thompson who trained and handled her in obedience and Nancy White who handled her in the conformationing. This bitch holds the *Dog World* Award of Canine Distinction in obedience.

One, Two, Three Goal

DECISIONS, DECISIONS. Before starting to obedience train your precocious puppy, your splendid special or your bratty brood bitch, do a little soul-searching to help yourself set good, realistic goals. A realistic goal is an attainable objective; a good goal is more than that. It should be challenging, and accomplishing it should give you a feeling of satisfaction.

To be attainable, a goal must take your lifestyle, attitude and dog into consideration. It's fun to imagine winning Best in Show and High in Trial with the same dog on the same day, but it isn't within the realm of possibility for most of us. The demands of breeding and exhibiting, the number of dogs you want to put obedience titles on and your job, family and other responsibilities must all be considered when setting goals.

If your dog puts her foot on top of yours when she "finishes," and you won't correct her because you think it is adorable, you don't have the attitude to set your sights on an OTCh. But you can still earn a UD. Just realize that each "points-off" mistake you make in Novice will intensify in Open and could become a problem in Utility. Your dog's foot on yours is only minor points off, so it is no problem in Novice where only one finish is required. But if you go on to Open, you will lose those minor points four times because four finishes are required. Sure you can still qualify, but your scores will already be lower than your Novice scores just on the basis of finishes. Utility will bring another drop in score because the exercises involve seven finishes. That's still okay, as long as you understand that what you train for is what you will get. If you allow your dog to stand on your toe when practicing, she won't magically correct herself in the show ring. In fact, the mistakes she makes at home and at class will be more pronounced amid the distractions of a show. So, before you set "qualifying" as your goal, be certain you won't be disappointed in your dog for obtaining no higher score than you prepared her to earn.

If you decide to set your goal at passing, don't let anyone make you feel guilty about it. The American Kennel Club (AKC) would not have set 170 as a qualifying score if it were not enough to show that your dog is intelligent and trainable. Breeders with specials, new puppies and several dogs to title may find that training multiple dogs to qualify is enough of a challenge and accomplishing it gives great satisfaction.

Some of you won't be happy unless you have given the best performance possible. Never proud of just being average, to you a mere qualifying score is tantamount to failure. Placements, High in Trial and OTCh. points have to be your goals. They exist, so you want to win them. But training to perfection could demand that you limit your obedience work to one or two dogs.

The dog you choose to train must also be considered when setting goals. While a five-year-old terrier may still be a youngster, other breeds, particularly some large ones, are feeling quite middle-aged and settled by their fifth year. A Utility title is not a realistic goal when beginning Novice training with a middle-aged "giant," although a few have probably managed it. When setting goals for brood bitches, consider that they will need maternity leave and aren't allowed to compete in obedience while in season. That doesn't mean they can't earn a UD, or even an OTCh. It will just take longer.

Goals aren't carved in stone, and dogs of all ages are adaptable, so if your goal is putting too much pressure on you or your dog, or is too easy to challenge either of you, just rethink it. Both of you will know when you get it right.

In the Ring Again

PERHAPS YOU KNOW someone who was active and intelligent during his working years but seemed to lose his vitality soon after retiring. Since dogs don't think as we do, they can retire young and live happy lives as long as they still get enough attention. The problem is they seldom do. And while never receiving attention will crush a dog's personality, there is one thing worse—growing up with star treatment and suddenly being reduced to an occasional hasty caress.

None of us wants to slight our brood stock, but our days seldom have enough hours and we don't get around to taking ol' Nell for a nice walk or playing ball with Molly. Never mind that ol' Nell is only four and Molly just turned three. They are retired champions and are inadvertently treated like underdogs. Nell's daughter enjoys the most attention, since she needs a major to finish and her coat and attitude are top priorities. Any extra time is reserved for socializing Molly's puppy. She will delight in her days of stardom as soon as Nell's daughter finishes.

Nell and Molly may be resigned to their second-class status by now, but Nell's daughter will soon be in for an unpleasant surprise. One day she will be groomed to perfection and pampered with her favorite treats. Then, if she wins the major, the best days of her life will be behind her, and she will join her dam as another well-fed, well-housed, semi-ignored brood bitch.

While it's hard to find time for a long walk or even a short romp, it's surprisingly easy to find ten minutes for ol' Nell when the time will be used to work toward a new title. And, sensing your renewed enthusiasm for her, Nell's tail will thump as she learns obedience exercises in return for praise.

If you are training outside with your dogs in runs, they will watch Nell enviously. Those kennel dogs would revel in the individual attention if you set up a schedule giving each of them ten minutes of training three or four times a week.

Your breeding kennel will derive many benefits from dual-titled brood stock:

- Puppy buyers will be impressed that your dogs' beautiful forms can function and that intelligence and trainability are in those typey heads.
- You may only try for qualifying scores, but when your dogs have obedience titles, people interested in obedience prospects will call you when puppy shopping, and some of them may be one-dog owners with the ability and time to work toward high scores. Eventually their pups, with you listed as breeder, could add to your kennel's reputation by going High in Trial or earning an OTCh.
- Obedience practice is good exercise for your dogs (and you), and well-conditioned brood bitches have fewer problems conceiving and whelping.
- For the same travel expenses you will have a second chance to make your show day successful. Check your premium list because some kennel clubs offer a cut rate for the second entry of the same dog.
- Many breeders charge more for stud service when their dog holds conformation and obedience titles, and puppies from dual-titled bitches may be in greater demand.

So, if being judged on the teamwork between you and your dog without regard for her type or color sounds appealing, if you would like more than two minutes of ring time after driving four hours to a show, if you often win the Breed competition and have nothing to do but wait five hours for Group judging, if you enjoy making friends with new people, and if you like the idea of setting your own goals with plenty of leeway and still obtaining a title, the sport of obedience can put the sparkle back in your old bitch's eyes and add a new dimension to your enterprise.

Selecting a Dual-Ring Dog

PREDICTING WHICH PUPS will mature into show-quality adults is just educated guesswork, even by the admission of respected breeders. Still, evaluating a puppy's conformation makes more sense than deliberating over an obedience prospect. Subjecting pups to elaborate tests really hasn't improved anyone's chances of finding a High in Trial winner, because your desire to work a dog and environmental factors play a huge role in your dog's scoring ability. It is just as common to ruin pups who tested great as it is to turn an unimpressive pup into a snappy obedience competitor. But no matter how hard you try or how well you handle your conformation dog, you cannot correct poor movement or lack of type.

Start with your breed standard and learn as much as you can about your breed. Attend shows and decide which families within the breed appeal to you. Then select a knowledgeable breeder who you feel honestly represents his stock and listens when you explain what you want out of a dog.

Whether choosing an adult or puppy, look for the following qualities:

- She is people oriented and likes to follow. She interacts with her litter-mates and explores new surroundings but does not become engrossed enough to tune you out when you call.
- She is confident around noises and, though she may hesitate momen-

tarily, will investigate objects like paper bags or laundry baskets, and then relax.

- You enjoy looking at her and find her character traits appealing. Later when you hit a rough spot in training, your dog's many fine qualities will stare you in the face and make waiting for progress easier.
- If you are considering a large or dominant breed and are unaccustomed to asserting authority, choose a pup (four months or younger) who allows you to:
  —Kneel next to her and roll her over on her back on the floor. It's okay if she struggles a bit, but she should calm down easily.
  —Take away food or toys she is engrossed with. The puppy shouldn't stiffen, growl or snap.

Ask the breeder if the pup's reaction to your handling is typical. If the breeder says the pup's behavior varies, look elsewhere for more predictable temperament.

Poodles, German Shepherds and many other breeds tend to be aloof with strangers, but they quickly develop a loyal bond with their owners. Therefore, they may be uninterested in following or playing with you. If you want a one-person dog or are evaluating a dog of any breed over five months old, make your decision based on whether she shows a lot of enthusiasm while interacting with the breeder.

When choosing a show-quality adult, look for confidence that stems from socialization outside of her property with children, adults of both sexes and other dogs. The dog should regard humans as friends and authority figures. A dog reared without rules will be a resentful student.

Select your dual-ring dog and breeder with the breed ring in mind. The most intelligent, trainable puppy ever whelped will not earn a conformation championship if her appearance strays far from the breed standard. But all your show prospect needs is normal temperament and a good training program and her success in obedience is up to you.

Getting the Most Out of Your Dog

THERE IS much to do, and much to learn, before you and your dog ever step into a ring.

PREPARING FOR THE RING

Building Rapport for the Shows

A flashy show dog displays independence, energy, confidence and intensity as she shows off her structure and character. Her handler acts as director, and she responds by moving, stacking, baiting and accepting examination on cue.

A good obedience program, one that corrects your dog's mistakes without berating her, will improve your teamwork in the conformation ring so you can bring out your dog's star quality. Working together on obedience exercises will help you read each other, and enhanced communication gives you an edge over the competition.

Confounding Communication

Have you ever misunderstood a judge's instructions? Apologetic as you may have been, he grumpily redirected you. Then, embarrassed and fumbling, you handled miserably. The judge may have thought you were stupid, but you wished he had spoken clearly the first time.

Even though we speak the same language, people often misunderstand each other. Communication is even more complex when we try to express our desires in "dog." We may think our dog is stubborn, spiteful or stupid, when the problem is our unclear instructions. Before blaming your dog for slow learning or a bad performance, consider how difficult it must be for her to learn from inept humans.

Awkward Ages and Stages

Be prepared to experience less than dazzling attitudes, speed and style during some learning stages. Many spectacular show dogs were hidden at home during the awkward adolescent period some breeders call "the uglies," and the brightest obedience dogs went through difficult stages, too. Miserable mental periods also occur during adolescence and are simply part of the learning curve.

Learning is stressful. No matter how slowly and carefully you progress, eventually your dog will have to try a new move or be challenged to make a decision. Give her time to work things out. You learned to babble before you could talk, so delight in your dog's initial successes but don't expect her first try to look like the finished product.

Learning Rates

Dogs, like people, have aptitudes for certain tasks. They shouldn't be categorized as slow or fast learners, because the rate often varies from exercise to exercise.

During Novice training a few dogs may seem to be truly slow learners, but with a persistent, patient trainer they eventually tune in. By the time they reach Open training, these dogs have often developed an average or even superior learning rate.

Blessed with Problems

Your dog's first reaction to training is not a good indicator of her real ability. Chances are you have overcome frustrating training dilemmas already. Who would believe your dog, who gleefully dances to the door when you pick up her lead, screamed and balked the first time she wore it? Or that prissy Missy used to potty behind the couch? Or that old Belle, snoring contentedly in her favorite spot, a crate with the door removed, frantically tried to burrow through it when it was first introduced?

Dogs who balk most defiantly at a new exercise can become great workers. The balkers resist direction from the beginning and try every conceivable trick to get out of doing it your way. If you make their resistance futile by showing them how you want it done every time they try to ignore or change it, they will learn that it is easier to go along with you and receive praise than argue the point and lose every time.

Cursed with Instant Gratification

Ironically, quick success often ruins a training program. When things move along easily, novice trainers may become sloppy and haphazard. Later, when presented with distractions, dogs who learned fast often lack real attention and comprehension, and the discouraged trainer has to start over, using a more careful approach and many distractions.

EVALUATING TEMPERAMENT AND STYLE

Temperament and style can change somewhat as you progress in training, so they should be reevaluated periodically.

Sensitive Sue

Timid, withdrawn types are so easy to baby; it's a shame that coddling is the worst thing you can do for them. When Sue collapses in a heap because learning is just too difficult, verbal consolation and physical attempts to mold her jellylike body into an upright form only encourage helplessness.

Instead, keep your pace lively and help her spirits along with a quick, cheery word, not lingering praise. Avoid direct eye contact and verbal corrections. Proof train exercises on lead until absolutely reliable, so that swift, silent corrections can be made without your hands touching her. Though normally considered a poor training technique, steady pulling corrections can build a wimpy dog's confidence. They are more directional than snappy jerks and less likely to elicit a submissive response. But if Sue becomes distracted, correct as usual.

Make congratulations and corrections short and perky, ignore helplessness and keep training. With a job to do, Sensitive Sue will have less time to be self-involved.

Defensive Duchess

Some dogs, particularly large, male working breeds (although it occurs in many breeds regardless of sex), can be defensive during training and must be handled cautiously to diminish the tendency. If Duchess generally behaves well around the house, doesn't pull on lead, obeys commands even when distracted, but growls and stiffens when corrected, she is a defensive dog.

When training a defensive dog, take extra time in the teaching phases. That will ensure better comprehension, so you will need fewer corrections. Always demand full attention by reverting to sneakaways if necessary (see "Sneakaway

Sessions'') before issuing commands. Correct calmly and deliberately by firmly guiding Duchess to make the right choice. Avoid eye contact, never scream at Duchess or rush into her and praise sincerely for a job well done. Once you have her attention, Defensive Duchess is easily motivated.

If your dog marks the house, challenges other dogs, is often difficult to control and also stiffens or growls when you correct her, you have a problem with pack order. Working on sneakaways will take the chip off her shoulder and establish you as leader.

Mellow Mable and Dizzy Dollie

There is no mistaking the laid-back or easily distracted types. They appear to have attended too many Grateful Dead concerts.

Keep Mable and Dollie on their toes during training. They must learn that if they doze or become preoccupied, they will miss something and wish they hadn't. Chatting monotone praise and giving ho-hum corrections will frustrate them. Move swiftly through your training sessions and praise as if you were cheering on the home team.

Corrections must be sharp enough to be effective and over in a flash. Quick movement, new challenges, interesting praise and powerful corrections will keep your laid-back dog from wishing she were basking in the sun and your distractible dog from looking for her kicks elsewhere.

Restful Rita—The Scrooge Complex

Some dogs hate work and will do anything to avoid it. If your dog is like this she is definitely capable of earning titles, but it will take a lot of fortitude for you to ignore her bad attitude and stay motivated. Rita will persistently put on a sour mug to remind you how much she resents work. She may hide in her crate when she sees you with a lead or run back to the house at every opportunity.

Amazingly, Rita can learn to like training and become a fine worker. But disguising work as play will never fool her. That's like hiding brussels sprouts in my hot-fudge sundae, hoping it will make me develop a taste for them. But biting into a vegetable when I expected sweets is more likely to make me hate my favorite dessert and distrust the culprit who tried to trick me.

Coaxing and bribery will not work with Resentful Rita either, so ignore her bad attitude and continue training firmly and fairly. Just as you may not be sure if you like a new sport until you spend enough time learning it, your dog will not enjoy obedience unless you keep her at it until she does it well. Develop your working relationship by following a well-structured program, praise whether she responds to it or not and eventually Rita will gain a sense of achievement, and possibly enjoyment, from her work.

DISCRIMINATION

Discrimination is natural. We couldn't survive without it. If you were not discriminating enough to assume that a speeding car would keep going through a green light, you might step into traffic and be killed. But some discrimination is prejudice. In our sport discrimination takes the form of assuming a dog will have certain limitations or capabilities because of her breed, rather than judging her as an individual.

Choosing a breed that frequently wins is no guarantee your dog will excel. If obedience were as easy as just picking the right breed, there would be no market for training classes, books, seminars and videos.

Picture Your Breed Hard at Work

Most people picture the ideal obedience dog working with her head cranked, feet prancing, tail wagging and eyes riveted to her handler. Few breeds actually work in that style, but it doesn't matter. Unlike conformation, where showmanship may play a vital role, obedience is judged on the performance of specific exercises with relatively little consideration given to how the dog looks doing them. Dogs who don't wag, prance and stare at their handler, but do work accurately and briskly, can also get high scores.

Watch the attitude and presence of your breed in conformation. Is it reserved or outgoing, docile or active, deliberate or agile? Develop a mental picture of the breed working obedience with that same style.

A breed described in its standards as "keenly aware of its surroundings" can give an accurate performance without gluing its eyes to its handler. But gaping around during exercises shouldn't be tolerated. A breed described as "dignified and aloof" may need more time and proofing to perfect the signal exercise, and the finished product will be a waiting look instead of an intense stare, but it will serve just as well.

Standards allowing a dog to be "suspicious of strangers" aren't intended to excuse fear in nonthreatening show situations. Obedience is a minimal test of mental soundness. Regardless of breed, a trained dog should not shy from an examination or refuse to walk around humans on the figure eight.

"That's Not an Obedience Breed"

When working an unusual obedience breed, be prepared for naysayers' uninvited comments. When you are experiencing difficulties, they will be there chuckling, "What did you expect with a . . . ?"

Just because your breed isn't commonly seen in obedience is no reason to expect your dog to be a poor performer. Work your dog with a good plan, not preconceived notions. If her performance falls short of your goal, look critically at your training program, not at your breed.

The Labrador Retriever, Ch. Green Valley's Spencer, CDX, JH, WC, owned by Benjamin L. Greene, D.V.M. and bred by his wife Linda, has distinguished himself in three competition areas. In adddition to being a conformation champion, he is obedience-titled and holds a junior hunter rank and a working certificate in retriever trials.

Conditioning Carefree Comes

TEACHING YOUR DOG to come when called—instantly and unfailingly—is essential to your training.

TEACHING THE COME

Eat and Run

When conditioning a young puppy to come when called, don't hesitate to use bribery. Introduce the word *come* at feeding time by saying her name, followed by "Come," in a happy voice. Show your pup her dinner dish, and when she follows you and the dish a few steps, praise and let her eat. Repeat every time you feed her.

Puppies love to chase, so use that instinct to your advantage. When your pup is very young, call her only when you know she will want to come—not when she is occupied with food, a toy or another person. As she gets older you will add distractions and enforce the come as a command. But not now. Touch your puppy playfully, say "Mancha, come," and run away a few steps while bending, clapping and talking happily to encourage her. Let her catch you, play with her a few seconds, then call her and run off as before. Three or four times is enough. Always quit before she wants to.

Come Is Just "Come!"

Always call your puppy the same way. If you use "Come" one time, "Here girl" the next and "Let's go" after that, your puppy may come in response to all these commands because your tone is inviting, but she won't learn the meaning of the word.

The Bold and the Bashful

There is no way your puppy can come and still be wrong, but some responses are more desirable than others. If your puppy comes bounding over, tail wagging her body, hug her and remind yourself how lucky you are. If she saunters over, when she arrives vary treats, praise and running away play to promote more enthusiasm. It is the puppy that lowers her body and kind of creeps over that needs some help. She may become even more submissive when she reaches you, keeping her head down and possibly rolling over and presenting her belly.

Many actors and even politicians were once bashful children, and your puppy's shyness could just be a stage. Don't rub that cute belly. Reassuring her is a mistake because it praises her submissive behavior. Instead, use the same happy talk you would use on an outgoing pup, but kneel when she reaches you and cup her face in your hands. Tickle under her chin. Get her to reach up for a treat. That encourages her to keep her head up and prevents her from lying down or rolling over.

On Lead Outdoors

Wait until your puppy is used to the lead before practicing the come outdoors. When she is walking beside you on a loose lead, call her and start walking or running backward. Cheer her on as she chases you, and reward with play and sometimes a treat when she catches you.

Canceling Your Conditioning

Suppose your neighbor invited you over for freshly baked brownies, but while you were contentedly munching, she steered the conversation to her allergies, wondered aloud if living next door to a dog owner was making them worse and launched into a history of her hypochondria. After she rehashed her rashes until the brownies became bitter, how would you respond to her next invitation?

After conditioning your puppy to come when called, don't erase your work by getting lazy and calling her over so you can push a pill down her throat or chastise her for "goofing" behind the sofa. *Go get her* for the unpleasantries, and keep her comes carefree.

Games Puppies Play

EDUCATIONAL TOYS for human babies sell well because parents know that while their children play, they are also learning how to understand and manipulate their world. Play conditioning is excellent for very young puppies too, and their games and toys aren't even expensive.

The ideal time to begin conditioning your puppy to become a dual-ring dog is as soon as you get her. Conditioning games teach your pup through educational play and will not put any pressure on her, so it is impossible to start playing them too soon.

Many pups are brave at home and in class but "come unglued" at their first show. These games, and variations you might create, should get your puppy ready to behave like a winner while assuring you of quality time together. Play conditioning a puppy is fun, but attempting to alleviate fears in an adult dog is a long, tedious chore, so a few games now could save you hours of frustration later.

Ignore the reactions that don't please you and encourage the responses you want. Games have no element of right or wrong, so don't give any verbal or physical corrections. Never reassure your pup when she is afraid. She may relate your cooing and stroking to praise and repeat her fear reaction because she thinks it pleases you. Praise her after she overcomes a fear and ignore her when she is timid.

CACOPHONY AND CONDITIONING

Human babies learn about noise when they play with rattles and other toys that allow them to control the amount and duration of the noise. Puppies will be more secure around noises after they, too, learn that they can create and stop a racket.

An empty plastic half-gallon or gallon milk container without a cap is a great noisemaker toy. It doesn't matter if the jug is bigger than your pup because it is lightweight and can be pulled by the handle. Lay the jug on the floor and watch TV or read a book. Let your puppy alone. She might have to overcome her fear of the strange object and may approach the jug and back off several times before touching it. Eventually she will become brave enough to drag it, shake it and bang it against table legs and walls. Like a small child with a toy drum or horn, she is learning that noise isn't so frightening because she can exercise control over it.

A loudspeaker that suddenly blares "Cleanup to ring five" could spook your dog at a show. Desensitize her to loud public-address systems by sometimes turning your TV or radio much louder than normal for a minute or two. Go about your business as if nothing were unusual.

If noise often frightens your pup, take a tape recorder to a dog show and record the sounds in the grooming area by a breed ring with a responsive crowd and during Group judging. Play it occasionally when your pup is resting in her crate, eating or playing. Start it a little softer than the sounds really are but work up to a realistic level. While it is okay to play it a little louder than it actually was, never set it uncomfortably loud. You want to get your pup used to dog show sounds, not make her dread them.

Give your puppy a safe metal toy, such as an old spoon bent double. Not only will it make a sound all its own when she plays with it, but when you reach Utility training she may be easier to train on the metal article than a dog who has never felt metal in her mouth.

Related conditioning activities include allowing your puppy to watch you blow-dry your hair and sometimes taking her picture with a flashbulb while she is eating or playing.

KEYS TO SUCCESS

Jingling and dropping your car keys can be a rewarding game because some conformation judges do it to check a dog's expression. Two times a week is plenty and will keep the exercise fresh in mind without boring your dog. On one of these drops, let a favorite treat fall with the keys for your pup to find. Whenever possible, have a friend do it instead of you. Soon the sound of jingling metal will prompt your pup to give the alert, quizzical expression all judges love.

COSTUME PARTY

A young dog, who previously showed with aplomb, can lose her confidence under a judge attired in a floppy sun hat or a rustling raincoat. The purpose of a "costume party" is to show your pup that while outerwear and accessories can change the form of the human body, there is still just a friendly person inside. Naturally, you will need a few "costumes." A trench coat, plastic raincoat, umbrella and large boots are a must. So are sunglasses, preferably with metal frames that glint in the sun, a wide-brimmed, floppy hat and a fake beard. You can improvise others and use Halloween masks if you have some. Invite children to play, but make sure they are old enough to understand the purpose of the game and won't try to frighten the puppy.

Begin with a single prop and let your puppy watch you put it on before calling her over for a pat and a treat. Don't suddenly appear doing a Dracula routine with flapping arms and a large cape or you could crush her confidence instead of bolstering it. Anytime your pup seems the slightest bit wary, get down to her level, busily tie your shoes or examine the floor and allow her to check out the scary item at her own speed without a word from you. Let her reach you and make the first move before you pet her.

When your puppy seems to enjoy watching you dress funnily, add props until you are wearing several items at once. Then add friends or children, also in "costume." When your pup takes the props in stride, begin walking a bit weirdly while wearing one of the strange outfits. Shuffle and make silly noises but sink to the floor and ignore her if your pup becomes frightened. When she is blasé about all the silliness, dress funnily out of her sight, casually walk past her and go about your business.

Play "costume party" outdoors when your puppy is secure with the game indoors. Try it in full sun and in rain since you could encounter both during her show career. Your pup should be introduced to adverse weather before you add costumes, but use common sense and never overheat or chill your youngster.

OBSTACLE COURSE

An obstacle course, sort of a puppy jungle gym, will help your puppy deal with strange footing and improve her coordination. You will need a piece of rubber matting for her to walk on, an old tire lying flat on the ground to climb over, some metal grating to negotiate (like a shelf from an old refrigerator or stove lying flat on the ground), three rug samples of various textures and a piece of waxed linoleum to teach her that some floors are slippery.

Armed with some treats and your puppy's favorite toys, place your props on the ground close to each other in a familiar area and put a treat or toy on each one. Then look busy doing something and let your puppy brave the footing at her own speed to reach the treats.

If your puppy is afraid of the props in a familiar area, ask a friend with a gentle dog or a puppy to let his play in the obstacle course with yours. Once two puppies are involved in play, you can put almost any type of strange footing near them and they will continue cavorting on it or with it. Breeders can condition whole litters by adding items of different footing to their play area. Just be careful they don't chew up and swallow the obstacles.

If your puppy is stressed by strange footing and you don't know anyone who can bring another puppy over to help out, set up an exercise pen and put a few samples of footing in it with a treat in the middle of each. Don't cover all the available space. Leave enough normal ground in the pen so that your puppy isn't scared when you put her in it. Ignore her and curiosity will eventually give her courage and she will reward herself by reaching the treat.

There is no need to praise a puppy who runs over each piece of footing right away. It is great if she acts as if they aren't even there, but play this conditioning game every couple of weeks anyway. Although she pays no attention to the different textures beneath her feet, someday when she is older and in a strange area, she may notice that the footing and the texture will feel familiar.

REST PERIODS—YOURS AND HERS

After a tiring day, you can collapse in front of the TV and condition your puppy for grooming and examination at the same time. Simply flip on your favorite show, put your puppy on your lap and pet her while you relax. But pet *all* of her. Touch her from the tip of her nose to the pads of her toes and, if she is a he, include the testicles. If your breed is groomed lying on its side, wait until your pup is fully relaxed and then place her on her side for petting. Later, change sides.

If your puppy doesn't want to be touched on some part of her body, don't pet that place continuously, but come back to it often with a cursory caress. This is quiet time, a time of pleasant communication through touch, not a battle of wills or a wrestling match. Keep your mind on the TV show and your strokes gentle and lazy and soon your puppy will be asleep. Now you can gently reposition her on her side to continue petting or concentrate on stroking the places she didn't want handled. Have you ever noticed that a new ring can be quite annoying, but after you wear it to sleep it feels more natural? It's the same principle.

Most kindergartens have a rest period sometime during the day. Your puppy also needs her rest and should be crated with soft bedding and a toy when she shows signs of winding down. Napping in her crate teaches her to be independent, and it accustoms her to the crate. Since she will travel to shows, stay in motels and possibly be benched in a crate, it is important that she become comfortable spending time alone in one.

If you play music in your vehicle while driving to shows, turn it on for your crated puppy or alternate music with a tape of dog show sounds. Soon she will relate a crate and music to nap time. Later, when you drive to the shows, your dog will sleep calmly in her crate and arrive rested.

22

GOING "BYE BYE"

Crate naps to music won't help your pup be a contented traveler if her only car rides besides the long highway trip to the shows end at the veterinarian's office with a vaccination. One short, pleasant trip per week should keep your puppy from relating riding to medical treatment. Secure her crate in your vehicle so it won't slide or tip if you have to swerve or stop suddenly, turn on the radio (if you usually do) and drive around for five minutes before returning home. When you have time, visit a friend who will fuss over your puppy or stop at a park where she can play.

LITTLE LEAGUE

Children learn coordination and social interaction when they participate in ball games. They also learn that cheers and applause are wonderful, not scary. Your puppy can similarly learn these things through ball games. Get your friends or children to help, and use a ball that is too big for your puppy to swallow but small enough for her to pick up. Roll it lightly, kick it gently and bounce it across the floor to each other. If your puppy tries to intercept, let her win sometimes, and when she gets the ball, clap and cheer for her. Allow her to keep the ball a few seconds, then take it back and continue playing. Quit before your puppy is tired.

ROUGH 'N' TUMBLE

If your puppy is very young or sensitive, win her trust before you play this game and add roughness little by little. But do try it. Extremely touch-sensitive dogs sometimes overcome their fear of body contact and learn confidence through painless but rough play.

Sit on the floor and pet your puppy. Then push (don't poke) her chest and slide her backward away from you. If she comes right back, tickle her and push her away again. An outgoing pup will catch on quickly and soon come bounding back for more. If your puppy doesn't return immediately, start over with petting and gentle play. The next time you push her away, slide her back only an inch or two.

Nearly all puppies like to play tug-of-war with a rubber toy made for this purpose, or a soft rag. But check with your puppy's breeder first because it may not be recommended for your breed's teeth.

MOUNTAINTOP

This game is intended for breeds showing on a table in the conformation ring. Obtain a grooming table or any sturdy table with a nonslip surface, place your puppy on it, praise her and play with her. Always watch her carefully to avoid a dangerous fall. Tickle her favorite places, roll her over and scratch her sides and belly if she likes that and put your face down to her to touch noses if she finds that amusing. Toss and catch a treat several times, then give it to her. Since you know your puppy, you will be able to think of other ways to delight her on the table and make it an enjoyable, not fearful place. Two or three minutes once or twice a day is enough. More is not better. Lift her down before she becomes bored.

THE BIG PLAYGROUND

The world is your puppy's big playground, and to function in it well she will have to get out and around as soon as she is safely vaccinated. While socializing your puppy to new places and people, always be on the lookout for special conditioning opportunities. Walking near a baby carriage or a shopping cart will prepare her for the loading dollies at a dog show. You may encounter revolving doors and elevators when showing in large cities, so introduce your puppy to them ahead of time, if possible. As you observe your puppy's reaction to each new experience, remind yourself: *Never pet her for being afraid* and *always praise her for being brave.*

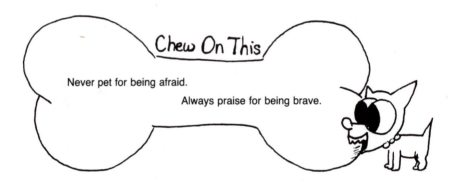

Chew On This

Never pet for being afraid.

Always praise for being brave.

Collars, Leads, Lines and Corrections

WHEN YOU BEGIN dual training, it is ideal if your obedience equipment looks, feels and sounds different to your dog than her conformation equipment. Later it won't matter. Once she is dual trained, your commands, tone and body language will instantly cue her, and she will be able to wear the same collar for obedience and conformation without becoming confused.

COLLARS

Buckle Collars

Some trainers, especially those with small dogs, use a rolled leather buckle collar for obedience training. For larger dogs they choose a flat, wider leather or nylon buckle collar. If your dog responds well to one of these, there is no reason to use anything that gives a more serious correction. Leather stretches and puppies grow, so check the fit every few weeks. While the collar should not feel tight against her neck, it should not be loose enough to slide off over her head either.

Choke Chains

Most obedience competitors use a chain training collar, also called the choke chain. Look for one that has small links, releases instantly and, when tightened, has one and one-half to two and one-half inches of excess chain before the ring attaches to the lead. The best-fitting ones are a little snug sliding over the dog's head. When worn correctly, the active ring (the one attached to the lead) will come across the top of the right side of your dog's neck.

The Prong or Pinch Collar

The dreadful-looking prong or pinch collar is not the instrument of pain it appears to be. When properly used, it provides a more humane method of correcting large, hard-to-manage dogs and is easier on the coat than the chain training collar. But it is not the collar of first choice. Although dogs often learn faster with a pinch collar, it can be difficult to elicit the same working ability later, without the pinch, because many dogs learn to respect the collar instead of the trainer. Use a prong collar only when your dog will not respond to either of the other collars. It is doubtful that you will need one this early in training (or at all) unless your dog is willing and able to drag you around, does not respond to or gags easily on a choke chain and has no respect for a buckle collar.

The prong collar does not go on over your dog's head. Instead, open it by pinching the links and sliding the prongs of one link out of the holes of the next one. Place it rather high up on your dog's neck with the section that attaches to the lead on the right. Close it by putting the two prongs back through the two holes. The collar should just fit, without excess looseness. If it is too large or too small, open it and remove or add enough links to make it fit properly. Before using it on your dog, try it on your own arm or leg. Then you will know what a correction feels like and see for yourself that the prongs are not sharp and do not damage your skin.

Leather buckle collars and chain training collars are permitted in the obedience ring; the pinch collar is not.

CONFORMATION LEADS

Various types of conformation leads are in vogue for different breeds and are worn in different ways. Watch your breed being exhibited, and you will see what the best handlers are using and learn the correct fit. Your dog's breeder may also have suggestions.

OBEDIENCE LEADS

You will need a lead that is six feet long and as wide as feels comfortable in your hand for training. Shorter, braided-leather leads have a neater appearance, feel nice in the hand and work well when you don't need additional length for teaching exercises. You might want to use one when you compete.

Holding the Six-Foot Obedience Lead

Place your right thumb through the loop in the lead handle and fold the excess length in your right hand so that you can remove the slack quickly to make a correction. Keep your right arm straight at your side with your knuckles against the outside seam of your right pant leg or hold your right hand against your right hip. Your left hand should stay off the lead unless you need to adjust the slack during certain exercises.

Left-handed folks may wish this training method would work with the lead in their left hand. It won't. But it all evens out in the end because lefties have the advantage when training for conformation.

Keeping Tabs on Your Dog

An eighteen-inch piece of three-eighths-inch diameter nylon cord folded in half with a knot at the end is used to form the right-side tab for medium-sized dogs. If your dog is quite large or quite tiny, you will need to adjust the length and thickness.

Slip the unknotted end of the tab through the loop in the collar. The knot should hang at your dog's chest. If she tries to play with it, correct with a "No" and treat the knot with bitter apple liquid (available from dog supplies dealers) if she persists. Put the tab on her during training sessions to facilitate more effective off-lead corrections. It gives you a "handle" on your dog, and the knot prevents your hand from slipping off.

THE LONGE AND LIGHT LINES

The longe line is a fifteen-foot nylon line with a swivel snap on one end and a handle at the other. It is used on sneakaways and intermediate stays, recalls, retrieving and jumping. The light line is a fifty-foot nylon cord that is tied to the tab. It is used to make the transition from on lead to off lead. For medium to large dogs, venetian blind cord works well. Smaller dogs need only nylon twine. If your dog is much faster than you and prone to running away, attach more than fifty feet.

A light line attached to a tab.

CORRECTIONS

A correction is strong enough when your dog responds to it the first time you give it by moving her body in the desired direction. If you commanded "Come," and your dog did not come, a proper correction would be a jerk toward you followed by an immediate release of the tension. Then praise. (Lead corrections are a quick jerk and a quick release—never a steady pull.) If the correction convinced your dog to get up and come to you, it was a good correction. If your dog ignored the correction, it was not forceful enough.

Having to repeat a correction over and over because it lacks authority is nagging, and nagging is much harder on your dog than one firm correction that works. But if your "come" correction jerks your dog off her feet or yanks her in your direction, it is too strong. A good correction should convince your dog to move—not be the cause of her movement.

Chew On This

A good correction should convince your dog to move . . . not be the cause of her movement.

The Newfoundland, Ch. Spillway's Refraf Argonaut, UD, DD, TT, TDI, is a dog of varied accomplishments. This talented giant has proven his mettle as a draft dog, and is temperament tested and a member of Therapy Dogs International. Roslyn Foreman is the owner-trainer.

Lead Breaking the Dual-Ring Puppy

WHEN LEAD TRAINING YOUR PUPPY, use a regular buckle collar even though she will wear a conformation lead high up behind her ears in the breed ring. During teething, puppies sometimes have sore, swollen glands that a conformation lead can irritate. After her permanent teeth have erupted, your lead-trained puppy will easily make the transition from a buckle collar to a conformation lead.

Let your puppy get used to the feel of a collar before starting to train. The first few times she wears one, play with her. If she is a chow hound, put the collar on just before feeding time. Let her wear it a little longer each session until she pays no attention to it.

When your puppy is used to the collar, attach the lead and allow her to drag it around. Keep an eye on her so she doesn't catch it on something and start struggling. When she becomes nonchalant about dragging the lead (or if she did not drag it because she was too busy playing with it), take her to an open area, pick up your end of the lead and follow your puppy wherever she takes you.

After your pup has enjoyed a few sessions of leading you, attach her lead to the doorknob and let her fight it out with a solid object instead of you. Stay in the room but ignore your pup for five minutes. She may scream and fuss, but if there is nothing she can get tangled in, she won't hurt herself. Try it once or twice a day. When she no longer has tantrums and knows how to relieve pressure on her collar, she is ready to go outside again. This time allow her to lead you for a minute, then begin putting gentle pressure on the lead and choosing the direction you both go. Walk toward, not away from, familiar surroundings, and encourage her with happy talk. Your pup doesn't have to be in any particular position—out in front, following behind or beside you are all okay at this point.

Gradually, as your pup accepts your leadership and becomes secure enough to walk toward and away from home with you, reel her in a little closer if she tries to pull you. When she walks near you on a loose lead, sometimes lean down to tease and play with her. If she still continues pulling, put the lead in your right hand and place your right hand against the front of your waist. Then put your left hand over your right to steady it. Pick a direction and start walking. Just as your pup is about to reach the end of the lead in front of you, make a quarter turn to the right and continue at the same pace. Do not warn or call her and wait until she catches up with you before talking to her. Then let her know you are delighted she rejoined you by happily saying something like, "Oh, there you are," as you give her a quick, playful pat.

Some pups lag instead of pull. If yours is still way behind you after a few sessions, turn to face her and run backward while clapping and encouraging her with your voice. When she catches you, play with her. If she is very young or small, allow her to catch you when you see her make the effort.

Five minutes a day is enough when lead breaking, and more than ten minutes is too much.

Sneakaway Sessions

WHAT'S THE FASTEST WAY to change a bratty dog's attitude, lead break an older puppy, teach attentiveness before obedience training and polish your gaiting pattern in the breed ring? First, stop talking. Then go the opposite of where your dog wants to go. Now you've begun sneakaway sessions.

Puppies should be twelve weeks old before beginning sneakaway sessions. They should also be somewhat coordinated; the less coordinated your puppy, the more slowly you should walk. Some pups can be preconditioned to walk on a lead by attaching it to a doorknob and leaving the pup tied several minutes a day. They may frantically thrust against the lead at first but will quickly learn to keep it slack when they realize that the door doesn't give in.

EQUIPMENT AND USE

Make or buy a longe line—a fifteen-foot nylon line with a swivel snap at one end and a handle at the other. Attach it to a snugly fitting buckle collar your dog cannot back out of. Put your right thumb in the handle of the line, and clasp your fingers around the remainder of the strap. Then place your left hand under your right so that there is no slack between your hands and the full fifteen feet of line is dragging on the ground. Hold both hands in front of you against your waist.

PHASE ONE: A LITTLE RESPECT

The objective of this exercise is to teach your dog to walk within five feet of you on a slack line, even with distractions.

Imagine standing in the center of a large Hula-Hoop with a five-foot radius. When your dog steps outside the Hula-Hoop, silently and swiftly walk away from her, and keep walking until she comes back into a five-foot radius of you. If she passes you and continues out of your radius, turn and walk in the opposite direction. Your dog will be jerked when the line tightens because she isn't attentive enough to realize that you turned. Never move your arms to jerk her. The correction will be stronger, more directional and totally objective when you keep your arms steady against your waist so that your full body weight powers into the line. Modify your speed to fit the size of your dog.

Resist the urge to issue a warning before the line tightens. When your dog can hear your intentions, she has no reason to watch. Likewise, don't praise when your dog comes into your radius. Staying near you on walks is not something you have to ask for and praise. It should become a way of life, an act of respect—like good housebreaking habits.

Why have your dog on a slack fifteen-foot line when your objective is to keep her within five feet? Holding your dog on a taut lead does nothing to teach her respect, attention and a sense of commitment to you. The long, slack line also allows you to build momentum so that the tug will be stronger when your dog lunges away.

Initially, the line may tangle in your dog's legs. Usually she can easily step out of her mess if you continue walking slowly, but occasionally she may get hog-tied. You will then have to back up to put some slack in the line, take a step forward to tighten it and repeat until your dog moves forward to loosen the line. Avoid returning to rescue her or she may try to tangle herself for attention.

Some dogs think the line is a wiggly chew toy. Discourage mouthing by having your dog wear the line a few minutes a day in the house and commanding "No!" when she grabs it. If she will not drop it, quickly spray bitter apple on the line or use a "scruff shake" by grabbing the skin on her neck while making eye contact.

Practice ten minutes a day for a week. With pups over six months old, you may speed results by training thirty minutes a day for two days before moving to phase two.

PHASE TWO: DISTRACTIONS

After a week, practice around distractions. They will teach your dog to ignore her impulses and remember her responsibilities. Using animals, children and food, practice in new environments like schools, parks or outside a kennel

When your dog becomes distracted, take off! Keep your hands against your waist.

Preparing for a lead-length sneakaway. The lead handle and the slack are in the right hand. The dog is edging ahead and not paying attention to the trainer, so a sneakaway is in order.

Attention-grabber. Sneak away when your dog is paying attention to a distraction. Holding your hands steady against your waist ensures an effective correction.

of barking dogs. When your dog discovers she can't focus on other things and watch your movements at the same time, she will become attentive.

Instead of walking, run away when your dog leaves your radius and stop dead when the line goes slack. When she is in your radius and attentive, saunter or stand still. If she doesn't stop in your radius, turn and run in the opposite direction again. Running makes the jerk stronger because you build more momentum. Don't try for track records when training puppies and small dogs.

After six ten-minute or two thirty-minute lessons with tempting distractions and jogging away, your dog should be watchful of your movements and stay near. If she lunges ahead, run directly out of her line of vision so she won't be able to see your actions peripherally. To build maximum momentum for correcting strong, stubborn dogs, start fast instead of gradually building speed. If space restrictions won't allow you to sneak away in some areas, avoid those places until your dog is ready for phase three.

PHASE THREE: REAL LIFE

Once you have obtained solid attention around a variety of distractions and convinced your dog to stay next to you on a slack line, you are ready to enforce the "no pulling" rule on a six-foot lead. Hold the lead handle with your right thumb and grab up the slack in your right hand. There should be no tension on the lead when your dog is standing at your left side. Walk briskly with your dog on your left and your right arm straight, knuckles against the right seam of your pants, so the lead runs in front of your legs.

If your dog tries to lunge ahead, open and close your hand so you drop the slack. Grip the handle, turn 180 degrees to the right and run as fast as you can until your dog is running behind you on a slack lead. Then fold the slack into your right hand again. If your dog passes you as you run, turn and go in the opposite direction until she is content to stay near you. Don't jerk the lead at all. Your body will do that for you. If running is not comfortable, walk with long, determined steps.

Your dog may try to walk directly behind you. Correct by shortening the slack in the lead, and be sure your right knuckles are against the outside seam of your pant leg. Walk straight ahead briskly, and the force of your left thigh thrusting into the lead will bring your dog to your left side.

Teach your dog to take leisurely walks on a loose lead, wait by your side courteously if you stop to chat and refrain from lunging through gates and doors. Allowing you dog to pull you around tells her she is the leader mentally and physically. Be ready to sneak away anytime your dog forgets the "no pulling" rule, because once you take obedience for granted, your dog will take you for granted.

Training with Drama

"MY DOG IS BORED," novice trainers frequently lament. "She's too smart for all this repetition." They are kidding themselves. The top dogs aren't bored in spite of constant precision training—not because they are stupid, but because their creative trainers keep zest in the rehearsals.

While people seldom dispute the importance of praise in a training program, they often assume play is contradictory to obedience. Ironically, few acts enhance your dog's sparkle and your team's rapport as much as the right play introduced at the opportune time.

PRAISE AND RELEASE

Knowing the difference between praise and release can give the dual-ring dog an advantage in both rings. Praise should mean, "Keep it up, you're doing great," while release is, "All done, let's play now." Consider the possibilities:

- In the breed ring, you can use praise to elicit a tail-wagging, happy attitude just before the judge looks your way. Without such training, a pep talk might make your dog wiggle out of show stance.
- In the obedience ring, you may not want to release an overly exuberant dog between exercises, but you can use praise to keep her spirit up while her feet remain on the ground. Laid-back obedience dogs need the motivation of a release between every exercise.

39

It is easy to teach your dog the difference between praise and release, and before long, you should be able to turn her "on" and "off" with ease.

Praise

Verbal praise should have inflection and interesting tonality. A monotone "Good dog" might be as much as a bonkers pup can stand in the initial stages of training and still keep all four paws on the floor, but for the majority of dogs, subdued praise is like elevator music—easy to ignore.

To discover the best way to praise your dog, talk to her with various inflections until you find a word, a group of words or a rhythmic chant that brings out her showiest expression. Just as we like certain songs and singers better than others, dogs often seem particularly pleased by a certain tone in our voice. A long drawn out "Gooood" or a cheery "Atta girl" tickles many dogs, but it is harder to find the right cue for some than for others.

A pat, stroke or tickle can also serve as praise, but your dual-ring dog needs to understand and enjoy purely vocal as well as physical encouragement. Keep hands-on contact brief. Excessive petting and stroking tends to put laid-back dogs to sleep and prompt crazy activity in excitable dogs.

Guidelines for Praising

- Inject praise when your dog makes key, good decisions. Use varied pitches and inflections. Instead of talking her through an exercise, use short, sweet and quietly enthusiastic phrases in between silences. That leaves her wanting an encore.
- Praise a hyper dog by first putting her on a sit-stay. Avoid eye contact and talking, but frequently return to offer a brief ear scratch. Leave immediately after the scratch, and since you haven't released, be prepared to quietly correct movement. Gradually introduce some calm verbal praise and eye contact, and show more enthusiasm as your dog is able to contain hers.
- Avoid using coaxing phrases like "Come on" and "Let's go" as praise. Inspire your dog with genuine congratulations like "Super!" or "That's it!" or "Whoopee!"
- Never soothe your dog while she is exhibiting aggression or fear. She will feel rewarded for acting the part of a thug or a wimp.
- Praise with intent to get a rise. Don't chitchat. Talk only when you have a point to make, or you will bore your dog and teach her to tune out and turn off.

Release

There should be no question in your dog's mind about whether or not she is released and may play. The first word trainers think of using is often a happy

"Okay," but that word could get you into trouble. Your dog might be sitting at heel when the judge points out a snag in the mat and warns you to be careful there. If you answer, "Okay, thanks," your dog might think she is off duty and begin playing. Sure you can tell her to sit again, but if you give that sit command with an irritated edge in your voice, it could put a damper on her attitude. So, before you choose a release word and cue, think about what you may say or do in either ring and choose a word or two that will not come up in ordinary conversation. A jovial underhand push on your dog's chest makes a good physical cue to use along with your release word.

FOOD

Although dogs respond to commands quickly when food is used as a teaching aid, the objective of a food-trained dog is to get food, not to complete the task. Just because a dog is doing an exercise doesn't mean she is comprehending it. Many food-trained dogs can't handle the stress of tuning out distractions and often have to be retrained to focus on work rather than food.

Trainers who use food must know how to physically manipulate their dog to make the right choices. When distractions or stress cause their dog to tune out food as a motivator, they still have to employ standard training techniques. If training with food, remember that praise is still important. Since food is not allowed in the ring, you will need praise to congratulate your dog and keep her spirits up.

For short periods, food training can work well to alleviate anxiety and improve attitude on trained, distraction-proof exercises. Use small bits of food your dog loves that can be eaten quickly and leave her wanting more. Never coax or bribe your dog into working. Make her complete the task to your liking, then surprise her with a treat sometimes.

PLAY'S THE THING

Praise is not enough to keep most dogs lively and willing throughout their obedience career. Creative games between exercises keep the spark alive. Imagine Pee-wee Herman as a dog trainer. Before training sessions got humdrum or tense, he might break off in childlike, quick movements and interesting chatter. He might occasionally face his dog and pounce, then run away in choppy mechanical steps, flop on the ground and cover his head. Soon the dog would poke its nose at Pee-wee's ear.

Is the dog fascinated with Pee-wee? You bet! Is she thinking about obedience? No way. That's the point. Without training breaks, most dogs get bogged down and flat. Knowing how to inspire your dog to play as well as work increases the bond between you, and the amusement relaxes your dog, making learning easier.

Play Guidelines

- Use play as a reward only after your dog has a basic understanding of the exercise. Otherwise she will concentrate on the toy instead of learning.
- Prolong play until after your dog peaks. She will feel tricked and learn to contain her excitement if the game always ends when she decides to participate.
- Keep trying when your dog is blah. Be more creative with your tonality and *move!*
- Play only when your dog isn't preoccupied. If she is distracted, work on attention by doing the "Sneakaway Sessions" (see page 33). It is okay for a dog to be uninterested, but it is not okay for her to try to find a better show while you are putting on the performance of your life.
- Add suspense after finishes and lineups. Softly sigh a drawn out "Goood" as you touch your dog on the fleshy part of her nose, and smoothly bring your hand back to your side. Then break off with a dynamic release as you step away and start playing. If your dog looks away at any time before the release, correct inattention.
- Never break to play while your dog shows resentment or fear. Improve rapport and communication through training until a bond develops. Then play. Otherwise your dog will look at you as though you were a used-car salesman promising the best deal in town and adding, "Would I lie to you?"
- Don't hesitate to add play to your training regimen because your dog gets too wild and won't go back to work. Nothing improves control with exuberant dogs more than instigating animated play and then redirecting their energy into obedience. Practice getting her a little excited and then giving a sit-stay. Have her on lead to facilitate quick, easy corrections. Gradually play harder and longer before going back to work. Giddiness in the ring can be a big problem with the high-spirited types unless you routinely switch from play to work during practice.

TOYS

Toys can be a tension reliever and a reward. Show and throw a toy the instant your dog completes a critical or difficult task, but not before.

Some trainers can even make toys boring. Don't simply play fetch with your dog. Tease her with the toy and encourage a game with interaction. Always have the lead in hand to reel your dog in if she runs away with the toy. Never try to pull it out of a clamped-shut mouth. If she clenches her teeth and refuses to drop it, begin heeling with some quick jump-offs at the start.

If your dog doesn't snatch up a toy, don't point at it and nag, plead or beg. Snatch it up as if you just stole a great prize. Then tease her by tapping it on the ground two or three times, sticking it under your arm and running away a short distance. Repeat several times before throwing it again.

Don't give up hope if your dog shows little interest in objects. Experiment with different types of toys and ways to tease. It takes several months to arouse some dogs' interest, but enthusiasm generally wins and most dogs eventually learn to celebrate when the toy comes out.

OFFER INCENTIVES, NOT BRIBES

Praise, play and toys should be offered when your dog completes a task, not to solicit a response. Keep your incentive out of sight until your dog does what you want, then present your goody with zest. Your dog shouldn't work like a donkey following a carrot. Tempting and teasing her into performing will make her complete the task but will not make her understand why she is doing it.

So what if you squeak, throw, run, push and pounce, and your dog sits quietly, looking down her nose at your antics? Sit on the ground and hug her, whisper in her ear, play with her paws. Soon she'll be leaning into you. Lie down on your stomach, cover your head with your arms, and she'll probably nuzzle your hands, lick your face and bond. Stay there a few minutes before resuming training, and take a second break before quitting time.

BALANCED CONTRAST

Dogs learn by contrasts in their environment. The better (not greater) the contrasts, the quicker the learning rate.

Training immediately after a period of separation from humans can increase the learning rate. It seems like fun in contrast to being bored and alone.

After she has been forced to do something she didn't want to do, your praise will let your dog know she finally made the right choice, and play will help her learn from corrections, instead of seeing them as punishment. Many dogs are more willing to play after fair, effective, well-timed corrections and remain more attentive for the rest of the lesson.

The American Staffordshire Terrier, Ch. Revol-Te Remercie Fraja, UD, is a winner in a weight-pulling competition. Her achievements are a tribute to careful training and to the great heart and strength of this breed.

Chew On This

Training the sit is actually teaching your dog *when* to sit.

Beginning Dual Training

T HIS METHOD will work on your twelve-week-old puppy, your two-year-old special and your five-year-old brood bitch. Just modify the training to fit your dog's age, size and previous work. If your dog has already shown in the breed ring to your satisfaction, you will be able to skip those sections.

Let's begin with some training rules:

- Train only when you are in a good mood.
- Watch your dog carefully when she is on a table.
- You, not your dog, decide when the training session is over.
- Decide it is over before your dog is bored or exhausted.
- Easy does it. Take your time.
- Motivate by praising all correct responses, except when instructed otherwise.

EQUIPMENT

Breeds that are examined on a table in the conformation ring should be placed on a sturdy table with a nonslip surface (a grooming table is ideal). Small puppies of any breed should also begin training on a table. After they learn an exercise, put them on the floor and go back to the first steps. Most of them will make the transition quickly.

Large dogs should be trained on the floor, but there are exceptions. You might train a large youngster on the table if grooming her has been a hassle.

Medium-sized puppies and dogs may be trained on the table or the floor, whichever is easiest on your back.

If you are training a young puppy of any breed or a tiny dog of any age, use a buckle collar for the exercises in this chapter. For all others, use a buckle collar or a chain training collar (choke chain), whichever works best for you.

SITTING AND STANDING

Are you worried about teaching your dog to sit because once she knows how, she might sit in the breed ring? Look at your dog. She already knows how to sit. Chances are she's sitting or lying down right now.

Training the sit is actually teaching your dog *when* to sit. That gives you control over your dog's sit. Once you have trained her to sit, down and stand on command and cue, she will know the difference between them and be more reliable in the breed ring than a dog who doesn't understand basic commands and tries to sit or lie down whenever she feels like it.

Early Training: Seven to Eleven Weeks of Age

A young puppy needs a stimulating environment. She needs to interact with other puppies, gentle dogs and humans of both sexes and different ages. She should be taught where it is praiseworthy to potty and encouraged to play with her own toys. She needs to explore new objects under supervision and feel grass, concrete and carpets under her feet. She does not need to learn commands like sit and stand. There is plenty of time for that later, so our sections on training puppies are meant for youngsters twelve weeks and older.

If you just can't wait that long to begin training your puppy, use the food method and introduce the sit and stand. To teach what "Sit" means, hold a yummy treat in front of her nose, say "Sit," and move the treat over her head so her eyes follow it upward, her head tilts back and her rear reaches the floor. Then give her the goody.

To stand her from a sit, say "Staaand," put a treat in front of her nose and move it forward slightly. As she stands, touch her right stifle with your left hand to steady her in place. The instant she is standing with all fours on the ground, give her the treat. Alternate practicing the sit and stand and she will soon respond to both words.

No matter how proficient your puppy becomes with treat training, start dual training as follows when she is old enough.

The Sit

Start a puppy with your right hand on her chest and her rear cupped in your left hand. Say "Sit" one time as if you mean it—short and firm, but not loud.

Your right hand pushes back slightly and slides upward to stop under your puppy's jawbone, where you tickle gently to keep her head up. At the same time, your left hand lightly pushes down and forward on your puppy's rear. Use the least force possible and give soft praise while holding her in position for about ten seconds. Sometimes give a goody after time is up, but don't let her see it until after she has remained compliantly in position.

When practicing with a small adult dog on a table, take the top of her collar in your right hand and place your left hand on her rear. Give the command and use your left hand as explained above while pulling mostly upward but a little forward on the dog's collar. The slight forward pressure should discourage your dog from rocking backward into her sit, a potential problem when heeling. Hold her in place for about ten seconds, while quietly praising.

When training your dog on the floor, stand so she is by your left side, in heel position, with her right shoulder even with your left leg. If she is wearing a buckle collar, follow the instructions for a small adult on the table. When using a choke chain, take the active end in your right hand, command "Sit," and pull mostly up but slightly forward while your left hand pushes down and slightly forward on your dog's rear. Relax the pressure on the chain unless she tries to move, then tighten only long enough to reposition her. You may have to kneel to keep her in place for ten seconds. Remove your left hand from her rear when her sit is steady enough so you can stand beside her and quietly praise.

Praising and Correcting

Keep praise for sitting, standing or downing low-key but happy (review "Praise and Release," page 40). Later, when your dog is gaiting or performing a moving exercise, your praise should be more stimulating, but during exercises where you command your dog to remain still, it isn't fair to overexcite her. If she tries to move before you release, stop praising, reposition her firmly and continue holding her in sit position for ten seconds without saying a word. When time is up, release her with your cue word and a friendly push, and play with her for several seconds. Practice the sit ten times per session, and sometimes withhold praise until your dog has remained in position a few seconds.

When your dog sits on command before you apply hand pressure, remains still for fifteen seconds while accepting occasional soft praise and responds playfully to release, she is ready to begin the stand.

The Stand

Begin with your dog sitting and the lead draped around the back of your neck so your hands are free. While "Sit" is always an abrupt command, the command to stand must also be firm, but pleasant and long. Say "Staaand" only once, then take your dog's muzzle in your right hand from underneath, so most of your hand is on the underside of her jaw, and pull forward slightly. At the same time, gently touch the area of your dog's stifle with your left hand. When she is on her feet, give soft praise as you steady her. After a few seconds release, play and begin again from a sit.

Gradually work toward a ten-second stand. If your dog moves before you release her, begin from a sit and withhold praise. When she is steady, praise again.

Always maintain your composure. Outlast a fidgety dog by matter-of-factly repositioning her until she succeeds.

Whether you have a puppy or a trained conformation dog, don't fuss with her stance at this point. Keep your right hand under her muzzle and your left by her stifle and you won't be able to pose her no matter how great the temptation.

Sitting for Examination

This is the first step toward the stand for examination, which your dog will perform every time she is in the breed ring and in Novice and Utility in obedience. Since dogs that are reliable on the sit for examination need fewer corrections to make the transition to the stand, it is best to start dual-ring dogs from a sit.

Start with your dog sitting by your left side or on a table and drape the lead around the back of your neck. Step just in front of your dog, cup her muzzle in your hands and look at her face and head. Then step beside her to your right (her left) and run your hand all the way down her back. Step in front of her again, tickle under her chin to remind her to keep her head up, go back to heel position, praise and release. If she moves during the exercise, give the sit lead correction— a light upward snap on her collar (just a flick of your wrist) as you push down on her rump with your left hand. As she becomes steady, make the examination more thorough.

Adding Friends and Neighbors

Give the sit command and remain beside your dog. Have a friend play judge and circle her until she doesn't react. Use the sit lead correction if she moves any part of her body except her head and tail, and instruct your helper to move confidently and avoid talking and eye contact. Next have the "judge" approach from the front, offer the back of his closed hand for your dog to sniff, and walk away. Finally he should pat her head, neck and body before leaving. When your dog remains still, praise, wait a few seconds and release. When you play with her after the release, let the "judge" play with her too. For variation, have two people examine her, one after the other.

Dental Delights

Teeth are examined only in the breed ring. If you are training for conformation, say "Teeth," and check them by gently pushing the top lip up and the

To use the slide down with a resistant dog, kneel behind her and grasp her legs. Then lift them up and slide them forward and down as you lean on her back and shoulders.

bottom lip down. Was that a problem? This may be the best time to correct it, but first, consider why your pup might hate having her teeth checked.

When you have a sore finger, you try to avoid shaking hands. When their milk teeth are loose and their gums are tender, many puppies don't want their mouths touched. If that could be the problem, put off examining your puppy's teeth for a few weeks and try it again when her permanent teeth are in.

Once your puppy has her permanent front teeth, begin conditioning by making the examination pleasant. Put your puppy or small dog on your lap for "teeth" training; sit on the floor or sofa beside your large dog. Have some soft, room-temperature cheese or liverwurst handy—something yummy and slightly sticky—and put a dab of it on your index finger. Say "Teeth," and as gently as possible (if she struggles it won't be gently at all), spread her lips to reveal her teeth, softly press the treat against them and let go. Repeat several times a day for a few days. This also helps dogs who are already showing in conformation but react to the mouth examination by rocking backward or worse.

When checking her teeth is no longer a struggle, put your dog on a sit-stay. Continue to use the treat, but enforce the sit with a lead correction if necessary. After she is steady, use the treat only occasionally and reinforce other times with praise. Teach a few helpers how to examine your dog's mouth and ask them to squish a treat into her teeth.

THE DOWN

Teaching this exercise may be extremely easy or horrendously hard, depending upon your dog's reaction. Some dogs fear and others resist being placed in a submissive position. Because dogs may react in so many ways, several methods of teaching the down have been developed. We will begin with the mildest and work up to the most forceful. You do the same. Give each method a chance before moving to the next one, and stick with the softest method that works.

Puppies and small dogs of any age may be trained on the table. Practice the down between ten and fifteen times a day. The command should be slightly long and given in a firm but soothing tone: "Dowwn." Say it only once, then enforce and correct it physically.

Slide Down

There are two ways to teach a slide down. For either one, begin with your dog sitting beside you on your left and drape the end of the lead behind your neck. Place your left hand on top of your dog's withers and your right hand behind her front legs, palm up. Keep your hand just below her brisket, not down by her feet. Command "Down," pause a second and push down and slightly forward with your left hand while your right hand moves forward, sliding your

Down with a push. Use your thumb and index finger on either side of the spine just behind your dog's withers (the top of the shoulder blades) to push her down.

Down with food. Lower your hand to the ground with food. As your dog's head follows, use your palm on her shoulder blade to push her down.

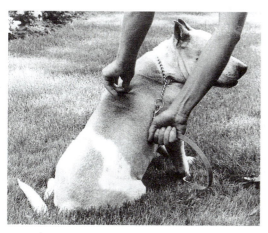

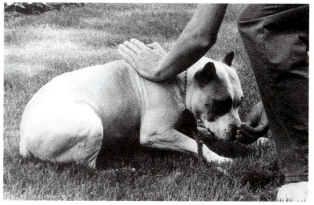

The jerk down. Jerk your dog off-balance by angling the lead next to her shoulder so that your hand ends up next to her elbow. Your left hand pushes as in the push down. Do it quickly and release quickly.

dog's legs out from under her. As soon as she is down, give low-key praise and keep her in position for about five seconds with hand pressure. Release and tell her she is wonderful.

For the second slide, reach over your dog with your left hand and grasp her left leg at elbow level while taking her right elbow in your right hand. Give the down command, wait a second and then lift both her legs up just enough to slide them forward into the down position. If necessary, lean on a resistant dog with your chest while sliding her front legs. Praise softly while keeping her steady for five seconds, release and make a happy fuss.

Always allow a second between giving the command and starting the slide. With a few days of practice, some dogs will down on command, so give her a chance to respond. Practice until you can easily keep your puppy in the down position for ten seconds and your adult for twenty seconds.

Push Down

Place the thumb and index finger of your left hand on either side of your dog's spine, just behind the withers. Command "Down," and push downward as firmly as necessary until your dog is lying down in any position. Praise while keeping her down for five seconds, release and play. Gradually extend the time down to twenty seconds.

Chow hounds who brace against the pressure can be downed easily by showing them a goody and lowering it until your knuckles touch the ground. As your dog's head follows the treat, place your left palm on her shoulder blade and push to the side. She will be so involved with the food that she will be happy to relax into the down as she gobbles.

Jerk Down

Use a chain training collar and sit your dog by your left side. Hold the lead in your right hand close to the snap and place your left index finger and thumb on either side of her spine just behind the withers. Command "Down," pause a second, then snap the lead down sharply at an angle so that your hand ends up by your dog's elbow. Your left hand pushes down at the same time. Practice until you can easily keep your dog down for twenty seconds.

The Anxious and the Angry

An occasional dog hysterically resists downing. If yours has this problem, review "Sneakaway Sessions" (see page 33) and work those exercises first. If she still resists, you need personalized help from an experienced trainer.

Hands Off

When your dog ceases struggling to get up, stop holding her down but keep your hands close to prevent her from rising before you release her. Gradually move your hands farther from her body but be ready to use them (not your voice) to correct immediately if necessary.

Test Time

After a week of practicing just ten times a day, your dog will have done seventy downs and been praised for each one. She should know the meaning of the command. If she does not go down on command, without physical help, by the seventh day, use the next more forceful training method as your correction. For example, if your dog spent a week learning the slide down, the next time you down her use the push down.

STANDING PRETTY

When your dog is accustomed to standing for ten seconds with your hands steadying her, she is ready to progress to a stylish conformation stand.

First you have to know what a stylish show stance for your breed should look like. When you purchase a dog from a show-oriented breeder, he is usually happy to demonstrate. But when your dog's breeder lives at the other end of the country, you will have to do some homework. If a book on your breed is available, it will probably have photos of dogs in show stance. You will see what type of leads they wear, if they are shown tail up, curled over their back or down, ears alert or relaxed and the myriad nuances that separate one breed's ring presentation from another's. The best way to see how your breed is shown is to attend dog shows. See ''Group Training'' (pages 65–66) to learn what to look for when learning to handle.

Some breeds are lifted clear of the floor, skillfully put back down in show pose and need little manipulating to look their best. If you have such a breed, don't let that habit carry over into obedience. You are not allowed to pick up a dog in the obedience ring.

A perfectly stacked dog is not a requirement in obedience competition. There, any stand will do, as long as the dog has good attitude and doesn't move.

STACKING

With your dog wearing her conformation lead, and without giving any commands at all, experiment with those suggestions that follow that fit your breed and your dog's structure. Stack her with quiet authority and talk pleasantly. Break often to play. If you experiment in front of a mirror, you may be surprised at how much you will learn about your dog's structure and your handling.

Most of the following suggestions are meant for the breed ring. The few you may find useful in either ring are marked by a *.

To correct a dog that leans toward you when you stack her, tap her ribs with your index and middle fingers.

If your breed should have a nice arch in its back, like the Whippet, but your dog stands so relaxed that her back looks flat, tickle her tummy (when the judge is looking elsewhere).

When your dog slumps so her topline appears to sag, tickle her tummy.

*When your dog's front feet fidget, steady her by placing your hand on her withers and exerting slight downward pressure.

*If your dog persists in lifting one front foot or the other, place the thumb of your left hand on the right side of her withers and your fingers on the left side. When she raises her right foot, press down with your thumb. When she raises her left foot, apply pressure with your fingers.

*Use your left hand when you set your dog's rear and place your right hand under her chin to keep her head up.

Try dropping your dog's front by lifting it from under the chest, allowing her front legs to dangle an inch or two off the ground for a second and then dropping them squarely.

*When a front leg is incorrectly placed, reposition it by lifting from the elbow, never the foot.

*Rear legs are repositioned by sliding your left hand down the thigh, grasping the leg in the area of the stifle joint and lifting or sliding it to the proper position. If your dog is small, or built low to the ground, reach over her to handle the left stifle. If your dog is large, reach under her to set the left rear leg. Be careful not to bump her belly or you could affect her topline.

To shift your dog's weight off a leg so you can easily move it, gently push your dog to the opposite side of the leg you want to move.

If your dog persists in roaching her back when you stack her, keep her neck high and her tail as high as the breed standard allows. Position her rear legs farther back than normal and stroke her backbone from the base of her neck to her tail.

To stop your dog from rocking back when you stack her, pull back lightly on her tail.

Stroking your dog under the base of her tail will teach her to hold her tail up. If you say "Tail" every time you do it, she may learn to raise her tail on cue.

When baiting, keep the bait low enough so that your dog's neck and head will be in their most attractive position. Baiting too high makes a dog look up and throws off her neck and topline.

Baiting is not feeding. Give your dog a taste of the bait just often enough to keep her interested.

With few exceptions, a squeaky toy is wonderful in the ring as long as your competitor is using it, not you. The dog who owns the toy is often bored with it, but the other dogs respond to the sound with excited attention and look wonderful. It is okay if your dog faces the opposite direction to see the toy. Just stack her in the proper direction when her turn comes to be examined.

Standing Alone

With your dog wearing her obedience collar and lead, give the stand command and stand her in a comfortable position. Your right hand should be under her muzzle and your left hand by her stifle. When she is steady, let go of her but keep your hands close, ready to stop her if she starts to move. Give soft praise and, after five seconds, release and play.

Practice until your dog will stand for ten seconds with your hands in sight but several inches from her.

Beginning Baiting

Switch back to a conformation lead to practice baiting. Once those treats are in your hand, don't forget to use verbal praise as well. A few judges will not allow bait in their rings, so it is important that your dog also show for praise and happy talk.

Start beside your dog and, with the lead in your left hand and your goodies in your right, keep slight tension on the lead and use the side of your foot to just touch your dog's right stifle or chest (whichever works best) to block forward motion. Placing your left foot under the stifle can also block sitting. Feed your dog a piece of goody after she stands still, attentively looking at you for several seconds. To increase the length of the stance, gradually delay giving the goody. Practice with a wall to your dog's left if she tries to sidestep and avoid the stifle touch. When your dog learns to hold an alert pose for several seconds, if it is "right" for your breed, begin standing in front of her, facing her. Hold the bait at a level that makes her look her best, relax your lead and use your left foot to keep her still.

The Puli Ch. Cameo Arrogant Advocator, UD, owned by Loretta C. Miller, is one of many in this breed to have successfully pursued a two-faceted career. *Kathy Upton*

The (Controlled) Brat

SOME DOGS are born hams. Show after show they stack themselves, cock their heads appealingly and flirt with the judge. But after several shows many dogs seem to find the conformation ring about as exciting as watching paint dry.

Controlled brattiness can get your dog a second look in the breed ring. Although the dog with the best conformation should win, and usually does, it isn't always clearcut. Two dogs in a class may be nearly equal and, when the judge has to decide between them, showmanship could be the deciding factor.

FLIRTING WITH THE JUDGE

If you are training an adult and skipped the chapter on "Games Puppies Play," go back and read the section, "Keys to Success" (page 20). Many judges jingle and drop keys to elicit a dog's most attentive expression.

At conformation practice, take turns playing judge with other members of the group. Before you do the individual gaiting pattern, give the "judge" one of your dog's favorite treats and ask him to bait your dog when you stop in front of him. Practice with several different "judges," and your dog will learn to stack herself in front of the real judge with an alert, expectant expression. Born or trained, that's showmanship.

While the person playing judge walks up and down a line of stacked dogs, he can occasionally hand one a treat. This should be done in no apparent order so that each dog continues to watch with anticipation but never knows whose turn it is. If a dog begins misbehaving when the treat is coming her way, she should not be rewarded. The ''judge'' can try her again later, when she is under control.

This one is for the specials. It only works in the Group ring or in a crowded ring at a specialty, where relaxed (not stacked) dogs are lined up around the ring while the judge examines and gaits each one individually. Although the judge is concentrating on the dog that is gaiting, he can't help but see those few dogs that are nearest the corner of the mat where the gaiting dog makes his final turn. The judge has to look in your direction when you are in the corner—in order to see the gaiting dog—but whether or not your dog remains unnoticed background is up to you. Be careful, however. If you seem to be trying to attract the judge's attention, it will annoy him. Always give the gaiting dog plenty of room. The idea is for you to do nothing and your dog to seem to be doing nothing. But she should be doing nothing in beautiful form, alert and responsive, simply watching the show.

To condition your dog to look great ''in the corner,'' have all the dogs and handlers at conformation practice form a circle, with one person playing judge. Each handler and the judge should have a tasty treat in his right hand. As one person gaits his dog down and back, the handler of the dog directly across from him turns his dog to face the oncoming one and whispers something that will become a cue, like ''Here he comes.'' The handler gaiting his dog slows down a little at the turn, reaches out and gives the standing dog a treat. The gaiting dog won't feel left out for long. As she returns, the judge will bait and treat her.

Soon you won't have to turn your standing dog. When she hears your whispered cue, she will look for a handler with a goody coming her way.

The standing dog and the gaiting dog must both be under control before practicing this, as they will be quite close to each other for an instant and a treat is involved. Each dog only needs one turn as the gaiting dog and one turn as the standing dog per practice session. Later, when your dog is ''in the corner'' at a show, whisper the cue word when a dog and handler move in your direction. Your dog will appear to be standing politely, but will look fabulous because she will be taut with expectation of a treat. When the gaiting dog is on its way back and the judge is no longer looking in your direction, you give her a treat.

You will get only one or two chances to look great in the corner before the line moves up and you are in a different position. Make the most of the opportunity.

PLAYING THE CROWD

Judges do not pick winners on the basis of crowd appeal, so applause won't make a poor dog win . . . but it won't hurt a good dog's chances. While most of the people at the breed ring are there to support a particular dog and nothing yours does will change their mind, the following suggestions could do you some good in the Group ring or in the extra-large classes that breed specialties draw.

When there are many dogs in the ring, you should release your dog so she can relax while the other dogs are being individually judged. But judges sometimes glance down the line of dogs. Although they don't expect the dogs to always be in show stance, it is never a good idea to allow your dog to mope around in the canine version of a slouch. It is best if she seems to be enjoying herself and better still if the good time seems spontaneous. If your dog's idea of fun is amusing to watch, she could become a crowd favorite and elicit hearty applause when it is her turn to gait.

"Catch" is a good game to play with your dog while she is standing relaxed. To look good, try it in the ring only after your dog consistently catches at least nine out of ten tries and loves the game. Some dogs learn to catch easily if taught with unsalted popcorn, perhaps because it is easy to see. Later, in the ring, you can use a soft, small toy that won't bounce, or you can use bait. Whatever you use, practice at home and at class first.

As long as your dog isn't disturbing any other dog, it is okay to have her do a trick if she considers it fun. Sitting up on the haunches and begging is a real crowd pleaser. Little dogs look adorable dancing in a circle on their hind legs. Dogs can be taught to balance a piece of bait near the end of their muzzle and, on signal, toss it in the air and catch it.

Training a dog to bark one or two barks on the command "Speak" can be useful, providing you can always stop her after the first or second bark. The noise is an instant attention-getter, so be certain that your dog looks wonderful when you ask her to speak, and don't overdo it.

If you teach your dog a trick, use it sparingly so that you don't turn your little section of the ring into a personal circus. Your dog is still being judged on conformation. But the word *show* is in dog show, and a bit of tasteful pizzazz can't hurt.

Choose a trick your dog loves and looks terrific doing, and practice it in training situations before attempting it in the ring. Your dog isn't ready for any extra flair if it excites her so much that she can't hold a stacked stand immediately afterward. Try to make games or tricks seem to be your dog's idea. If you can make your dog believe that too, so much the better.

Watch Group judging whenever you have the opportunity. You won't see these tricks very often because they take time to train, must be subtle to work and are not necessary to win. But when you do see a dog do something that gives it a little edge, it is often unforgettable.

The Briard, Ch. Brie-Zee Princess Tribble, owned by Julie Treinis holds the UDTX degree in the U.S. and Canada and the UD, TT and VT titles in United Kennel Club and States Kennel Club trials. She is shown here having some casual fun with her owner, using her for the high jump.   *Marlene Bryant*

Chew On This

Training isn't what we try to teach—it's what our dog learns.

The Trainer as
Benevolent Dictator

$\mathbf{F}$ROM EARLIEST PUPPYHOOD, your dog learned that certain behaviors, like when and how hard to play and nurse and where to go potty, were strictly enforced during pack life with her mom and littermates. So don't feel bad about making and enforcing household rules. Without limitations, dogs become confused and neurotic. Like an indulged child who throws temper tantrums to manipulate his parents, stubborn dogs are usually just using the tried-and-true method you taught them to get their way: Resist long and hard.

The more rules you enforce, the more freedom your dog will eventually enjoy. Well-mannered dogs are good travelers and don't have to be crated when you have guests.

LET YOUR HANDS DO THE TALKING

Dogs learn by doing, not talking about it. Observe professional handlers working unfamiliar dogs at the shows. They make their point by using firm hands and body language to manipulate dogs into positions that make them settle down, show off or engage in play. Dogs are action oriented, so watch, experiment and learn how to speak with your hands.

BALANCING ACT

Try to balance work, play, togetherness and detachment.

We cherish our dogs, and pampering them makes us feel good. But well cared for and indulged are two different things. Dogs must rely on us for everything—food, exercise, play and potty breaks. No wonder our faithful companions often believe humans were put on earth to be their servants.

Choose the time and place to feed, potty, exercise, play and train. Sometimes your dog may remind you, but don't let her dictate. "Read" whether she is demanding attention or has a real need. Maintain a life of your own and give your dog the space and time to be a dog. Let her romp in a safe field, play with other dogs, chew on a toy and engage in fun activities without your interference.

Just because your dog is bonded to you does not necessarily mean the two of you have a good relationship. Some dogs and owners are neurotically over-bonded. Panicking whenever you leave isn't a sign of devotion—it is irrational, compulsive behavior. Leave your puppy alone and safely confined for an hour or two every day so she will learn that no matter where or when you leave her, she is safe and must be quiet. While she may not exactly be relaxed, at least she should not be upset. Socialization interspersed with separations develops confidence and character while discouraging obnoxious, demanding attitudes. They also enable your dog to work with a handler and adapt to boarding.

COMMUNICATE CONSISTENCY

To build trust, communicate your desires to your dog in a consistent language, both verbal and nonverbal. Enforce, don't nag. Your dog will become more stable once she knows that (1) you won't ask for more than she can give, and (2) if she doesn't understand or doesn't want to, you will immediately show her what you had in mind.

You control whether or not your dog is allowed to develop a bad habit. Let her know when you like what she is doing and when you disapprove, and be careful that bad habits are not reinforced when you are away through lack of confinement or improper supervision. Be fair to your dog. Persist in eliminating her annoying habits so that your frustration doesn't build to where you dislike being with her because of poor behaviors you failed to correct.

Nothing kills a good training program quicker than bogus commands. Say what you mean and mean what you say. Bogus commands come in four varieties:

Nonsense: Don't say, "Come on now, sit down," while you are grooming and expect your dog to respond. Give a real command once ("Sit") and enforce it.

Ignored: If you tell your dog to sit at the veterinarian's office but allow her to continue meandering because you are too busy socializing to enforce, she just learned that "Sit" means nothing.

Yelling or pointing: Have you ever been on the phone with someone who excuses herself and screams, "Shut up!" at the top of her lungs because her dog is barking incessantly? If your dog only responds to a scream, teach her to obey a normal tone by correcting immediately after the first command instead of after screams. Dogs who respond only to shouting have learned that this is the only time their owner cares enough to enforce.

Repeating: Impress upon your dog that what you say is important. If she doesn't understand a command, repeating won't make the meaning any clearer. Physically guide her into obeying the command if she is confused. Enforce the command with a correction if she understands but refuses.

When you doubt your ability to reinforce a command, it is better not to give it than allow it to be disobeyed. Training isn't what we try to teach—it is what our dog learns, and unintentional training shapes our dog's behavior more than formal practice sessions.

Don't worry if family members give bogus commands. It won't destroy your training. Dogs quickly learn who means it and who doesn't.

The English Cocker Spaniel, Ch. Rustlin Puttin' On the Ritz, UDT, owned by Sally Culley—as photogenic as he is accomplished.

Group Training

CLASSES IN OBEDIENCE, conformation or both are often offered by dog clubs and are also available through privately owned training schools. Besides being fun and designed to catch your handling errors, class work gets your dog used to working with strange dogs, people and noise.

Since there is no such thing as a certification test for dog training instructors, programs range from excellent to awful. It is easier to find a good instructor when you know what to look for.

SELECTING A CONFORMATION CLASS

To present your dog skillfully in the conformation ring, you have to consider her breed as well as her virtues and faults. Begin by studying your breed standard and attending dog shows as a spectator. Watch the handlers manipulate the dogs, and note the most popular or traditional way to exhibit your breed. Study the difference between a fine presentation and a mediocre one, and watch breeds similar to your own until you have a mental image of the ring presence you wish to achieve. It is a good idea to remain for Group judging and notice how the top handlers make their craft look easy and never overhandle.

Before you sign up for a conformation class, ask to observe a session. Don't expect the students to be polished handlers, but see if the instructor makes helpful suggestions or just calls commands and examines dogs without offering advice. Do students who need it receive individual attention? Are the dogs and handlers enjoying themselves, or do they appear bored and tired? Is the examination a pleasant or at least a neutral experience for the dogs? If the instructor seems knowledgeable and the dogs are treated warmly, praised frequently and appear animated, the training class will probably prove useful. Once you join, don't overwork a young puppy. Drop out of the line before she is exhausted.

SELECTING AN OBEDIENCE CLASS

Before choosing an obedience class, see dogs compete at a match or show. Then watch several classes before enrolling. There are many methods of teaching obedience, and it is important that the program be compatible with your beliefs and goals. Are new exercises taken apart and taught piece by piece with a sensible progression toward the whole? Is the instructor creative, or are the exercises drilled over and over without variation? Do all students receive individual attention when they need it, or does the instructor only pay attention to those with exceptional talent and typical obedience breeds? Does the instructor compete in obedience? One way to determine a good school is to discover whether it produces titled dogs of various breeds and sizes with handlers of all ages. If most of the dogs appear to be willing workers, praise is a major training tool and you feel comfortable with the trainer and his methods, the class will probably be fine for you.

When you join, don't ask permission to work your dog differently from the rest because she is a "breed" dog. The regular lessons will not confuse her, and the heel and sit practice will not carry over into the breed ring unless you fail to review conformation techniques.

THE LONE TRAINER

If no classes are available in your area, continue training your dog "by the book." But start looking for kindred spirits because, without group practice, very few dogs will remain attentive to their handler when surrounded by strange dogs and a crowd of people. Ask local veterinarians, groomers and boarding kennel owners if they can help you locate people who show their dogs. If you find just a few people to work with, you can take turns examining each others' dogs, and the dogs can practice sits and downs together. Set aside the same evening each week for cooperative dog training, think of ways to help each other over rough spots and before long you won't need a training club—you will be one.

Using the Green and Blue

IN THE CHAPTERS THAT FOLLOW, ''Earning the Green'' explains how to earn qualifying scores with a dog who is reliable but sloppy. After building a good foundation with the ''Green'' you may want to increase precision by practicing the ''Turning it Blue'' techniques. While the ''Green'' dog will just earn titles, the ''Blue'' enthusiast may collect placements, trophies, special club awards and national recognition.

This book basically covers the exercises in the order they are performed in the ring. But when you train, teach all the commands for that class on lead before beginning off-lead training on any of them. It makes no sense to spend time perfecting an off-lead recall with a dog who can't do an automatic sit.

Although you can't show in Open until you have a Novice title, there is no reason why you can't train your dog to do advanced exercises as long as she knows the prerequisites listed at the beginning of that exercise. Think how confident you'll be on Novice stays if your dog is flawless on out-of-sight stays, or what a cinch the recall will be once you've mastered hand signals.

There are many different ways to complete any job, and dog training is no different. This book doesn't attempt to explain every successful technique. If it did, each exercise would be a book in itself.

When a technique is unsuccessful, a book can't correct your interpretation or timing, and that could make all the difference. If you are stumped by a problem, there is no substitute for a knowledgeable mentor.

NOVICE:
Earning the Green

Where Are the Lead Jerks?

OUR HEELING METHOD uses body movements, particularly giant steps, turns and jumps, to tighten the lead. There are lead jerks in our method; we just don't use them when teaching heeling, except for correcting the sit. This has several advantages for the dual-ring dog:

- Since you will simply be moving, not obviously correcting, your dog will feel responsible when she receives a correction instead of attributing it to you.
- The way the lead is held is so far removed from conformation that many dogs won't even be confused in the earliest stages of training.
- When trainers are responsible for giving lead-jerk corrections, their frustration sometimes shows through the lead. But when your lower body makes the correction automatically, your patience and cheerful attitude will not be tested.
- Since dogs like to run and chase, your dog's attitude will improve with every correction.
- Your dog will learn to watch your body, not out of nervousness, but because she has learned that she can control whether she is corrected or not.
- When she is in heel position, your dog will never receive a badly timed jerk.

- Afraid you're not athletic or coordinated enough to jump? It takes much less practice to giant step or puddle jump than to give good, sharp, well-timed lead jerks.

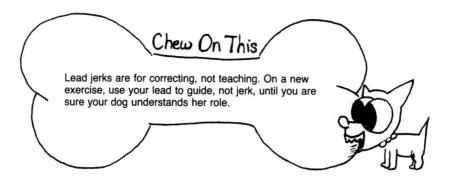

Chew On This

Lead jerks are for correcting, not teaching. On a new exercise, use your lead to guide, not jerk, until you are sure your dog understands her role.

Heeling on Lead

Prerequisites

Review "Sneakaway Sessions" (see page 33). Heeling is more precise than gaiting or just walking willingly on lead, so your dog should be attentive and distraction-proof. She should also sit on command and know what "Stand" means. If these are a problem, review those sections of "Beginning Dual Training" (see page 45).

What's New?

Heeling is always your first exercise in the obedience ring. Unlike conformation, whereas the judge usually stands in one place while your dog gaits, the obedience judge will walk near you and call out commands.

Relationship to Conformation

Most dogs who sit during breed judging don't know any better, but your dog won't be one of them. After she learns automatic sits and heeling into a stand, she will be aware of the difference, and you will have control of both responses.

Equipment

Obedience collar and lead.

Teaching the sit while heeling. Tighten the lead as you halt, and give the sit command as you pull upward on the lead and press down on your dog's rump. You may turn toward your dog slightly for better control and leverage.

When your dog fails to sit, correct with an upward jerk directly over her head.

Chew On This

REQUIRED READING

Play by the rules. Get them free from the AKC. Write to the American Kennel Club, 51 Madison Ave., New York, N.Y. 10010 and request the *Obedience Regulations*.

REQUIRED READING

TEACHING THE EXERCISE

Part One

Begin with a taut lead in your right hand (no slack and slight pressure). Your dog is sitting in heel position (dog's right shoulder even with your left leg).

Say your dog's name and "Heel" in a cheerful tone and step off on your left foot. Never repeat the word *heel* until you begin again from a sit.

Walk at a normal, brisk pace and turn in the opposite direction when your dog tries to leave heel position. If she looks or veers left, make a quarter turn to the right. When she crowds or bumps you, make a quarter turn left, into her. If she lags or doesn't give you full attention, surprise her by jumping forward. If she tries to pull ahead, sneak away by dropping the slack and making a 180-degree right turn. Praise enthusiastically immediately after every jumping or turning correction.

Your body movements should not be dramatic at this point because your dog is just trying to figure out heel position. If you hold your lead with enough tension on it, she can't make much of a mistake anyway.

When you halt, give the sit command and sit your dog by putting upward tension (not a jerk) on the lead and pressing down on her rump or left hip (no harder than necessary) to guide her into a straight sit.

After your dog seems to understand heel position, try left and right quarter turns, large circles and smaller circles in both directions. Zigzag around and between objects, change your pace to slower and faster and practice 180-degree turns to the right and left. Even though your lead should be taut enough so that she can hardly go wrong, praise her following every curve or turn.

Part Two

When your taut lead seldom becomes a tight one, it is time to put some slack in it and hold it properly. Keep the lead in your right hand with your knuckles against the seam of your pants or on your right hip and you won't be able to make an ill-timed or improper correction. Kept in this position, the lead will hit your upper left thigh with a steady pull when you turn or jump to correct, and the result will be a properly timed, directional correction.

Practice heeling the same way as in part one, using turns, circles, changes of pace and zigzags. Add plenty of distractions, like other dogs, people, toys and treats on the ground and practice in new locations. Your corrections will be strong now because slack in the lead gives you more leverage and allows your dog to get farther out of position. Always praise immediately after every correction.

Continue to give the sit command as you halt but jerk the lead upward now to achieve a quick, straight sit. Guide your dog's rear with your left hand if necessary.

Caution: Do not let the lead fall below your knee or you will overcorrect your dog and probably trip.

Part Three

Repeat everything as you did it in part two with two exceptions: stop giving the sit command when you halt (use lead corrections silently if necessary), and make your turns and jumps more dramatic so that your dog will receive a stronger correction. Be creative with your distractions, and plant a few more each practice session. Work in as many strange places as you can, praising often and enthusiastically.

Walking into the Stand

Once your dog sits automatically when you halt, teach her to walk into a stand. She won't have to use it in the obedience ring until Utility, but it is handy in the conformation ring.

Heel a few steps and, just as you halt, command "Staaand." Signal with a sweeping motion of your right arm in front of your dog's eyes and chest and gently touch her stifle with your left hand. Tickle under her jaw and praise. Eventually she will stand for the hand signal and you won't need to touch her stifle or give the verbal command.

Common Errors of the Dog and Simple Corrections

Poor starts. Set up a good distraction and when your dog is fascinated by it, command "Mancha, heel," turn right abruptly, move out quickly and praise. This teaches your dog to watch and be ready fast.

Lagging, sniffing and inattention. Make sure your dog has no tendency to balk when the lead tightens. If she does, review sneakaways (see "Sneakaway Sessions," page 33). Later, correct lagging by stepping a quarter turn right with your right foot and jumping forward with your left leg leading—like jumping over a puddle.

Lack of attention. The instant your dog glances away while heeling, turn the opposite of where she is looking and jump forward in the new direction. Stop practicing heeling to review sneakaways whenever your dog becomes fascinated by your creative distractions.

Heeling wide (dog too far from your leg), turning wide and lagging on turns. Perform another puddle jump. This time make a quarter turn to the right on your left leg, step out on the right, then jump forward with your left. The same correction works on dogs who lag after left turns. Simply change it to a quarter turn left (use the same footwork, no need to reverse it).

Jumping into the lead to correct lack of attention. When the lead is in your right hand with your knuckles against the outside seam of your right pant leg, it pulls across your left thigh to correct your dog.

The "Jackie Gleason left turn." Get better balance and prevent your dog from hopping right by holding the lead taut in your left hand.

Maintain your balance by leaning forward so that your shoulder is over your knee.

Finish the "Jackie Gleason left moving your left foot under your dog's front legs.

Going too wide on about-turns. Following an about-turn, step out on your right leg in the new direction and jump forward with your left.

Forging (in motion and on the sit), crowding, bumping and sniffing (use only on dogs larger than toy size). The "Jackie Gleason left turn" is handy for correcting medium and large dogs. Pivot left on your right leg and bend slightly at the knee and waist as you take an "and away we go" step into your dog so that your left foot steps behind her front legs. If your dog tries to jump in front of your legs or to the right (instead of skirting back to the left), take up the slack in the lead but don't jerk her.

Forging and crowding (any size dog). Make a quarter turn left or a left U-turn.

No change of pace or not enough change of pace. Use the same corrections as for lagging or forging at normal speed.

Sniffing. Mix up all the corrections used for forging and lagging and sometimes halt and give an automatic sit correction. Your dog will soon learn that she gets a correction every time she sniffs, but she won't know which one.

Crooked sits. Poor sits are usually caused by lack of attention, so don't practice halts when your dog is distracted. Instead, correct lack of attention with a right turn and a jump forward. If your dog still sits crookedly, go back to sneakaways until she wants to watch you.

If your dog is attentive and quick but still sits crookedly, use your left hand on the lead (above and to the right of her head) to angle her into a straight sit. Praise by petting her right cheek to encourage looking up and sitting straight. A karate chop motion against your dog's left thigh just before she sits will straighten out her rear.

If your dog sits with her rear behind your leg, automatically place your right foot behind your left as a block. Never lift your foot to tap or kick her, as she will become wary and overcorrect.

No sits. Upward jerk and release. If necessary, use two hands with a strong dog.

IN THE RING

Responsibility of the Dog

- Remain in heel position during left, right and about-turns and at different speeds on the straightaways.
- Sit automatically when handler stops.

Responsibility of the Handler

- Use correctly fitting equipment on your dog.
- Wear no clothes or jewelry that distracts or interferes with your dog.

- Keep a loose lead.
- Make smooth but obvious changes of pace.
- Maintain a natural posture. Do not look over your shoulder to watch your dog lag.
- Issue a clear command, only once, each time the judge says, "Forward."
- Maintain steady arms and hands. Jiggling could be interpreted as a second command.

Common Handler Errors and Simple Corrections

Stepping into your dog on automatic sits. This is one of the most frequent errors in the Novice ring. The handler tries to get closer to his dog, the dog has to make room for the handler's left foot—and what might have been a straight sit isn't. Ask a friend to watch you from behind. If you are guilty, practice starting and stopping several times without your dog. Beware: People who make this mistake tend to correct it at practice but regress in the ring.

Maintaining a tight lead. Let more lead out if your dog lags a little or you will lose points for a tight lead besides the lagging. If all your lead is out and she's hanging back at the end of it, you probably entered the competition before she was ready. Chances are she will turn into a spectator on the heel free and join the judge to watch you do the pattern.

Adjusting your pace to your dog's. The rules say you should walk "briskly and in a natural manner." There are exceptions. A basketball player would be wise to walk his Chihuahua naturally and ignore the word "briskly." No dog should have to heel at a gallop, but there is nothing wrong with expecting your dog to trot smartly. Don't slow down to accommodate a lagging dog or speed up to stay with a forging one. If you practice that way your dog won't learn to heel, but you will. Judges recognize that syndrome in a heartbeat. There is a place on the score sheet to mark "Handler continually adapts pace to dog." It is one of the first items under the heading "Non-Qualifying Zero."

Changes of pace too jerky or not definite. Although you are expected to change pace quickly on the judge's command, you don't have to squeal into the slow or take off as if it's a race. Slow down considerably on the slow and run on the fast, but move into them smoothly so that your dog will be able to stay in heel position. Practice smooth changes of pace without your dog first. Have someone else call the slow, normal and fast commands, or make a recording of yourself calling commands at various intervals. Trying to call them for yourself as you practice them never works because your feet behave better if they know when the command is coming.

Weaving. Try this with a friend. Draw a straight chalk line on the pave-

ment. Have your friend play handler and walk down the line while you play dog and walk beside him on his left. Try to maintain heel position as he speeds up, slows down and does about-turns, all smoothly but without warning. You may discover that heeling isn't terribly difficult. Try it again without a line on the ground and tell your friend to weave from side to side just a little. How easy is the dog's role now?

At outdoor shows where there are no mats, line up with a stationary object at the other end of the ring and aim yourself toward it. No dog can gait or heel well if her handler meanders.

Name that gait. Some handlers go to amusing lengths to cover up for a dog that doesn't do the fast well. To appear fast when they are not, they bounce up and down almost in place by lifting their knees high and kicking backward with their feet. No one is fooled, but everyone grins, especially the gremlins.

Repeating the heel command. Whether to issue a second command to heel or while heeling is a judgment call. If something distracts or spooks your dog and she doesn't recover, it is worth a try. She will lose points, but you may save the exercise.

Passing

Keep slack in your lead, make no physical or verbal corrections and don't adjust your speed to your dog. If she doesn't balk or try to leave the ring, is in heel position more often than not and sometimes remembers to sit when you halt, she will probably pass.

Chew On This

Twenty minutes of obedience training a day, five days a week, is about right for most adult dogs. Always gauge your dog's attitude. Some days less is better than more.

Figure Eight on Lead

Prerequisites

Your dog should heel happily and attentively. When she adjusts her speed on the slow and fast without corrections and you have resisted the temptation to adjust yours, both of you are ready to learn the figure eight.

What's New?

To maintain heel position on inside and outside turns, your dog must make abrupt changes of pace while your speed remains steady. She also has to heel around and sit beside strangers without becoming distracted.

Relationship to Conformation

Learning to circle in the relatively tight figure eight area will give a large dog more flexibility. That translates to smoother triangles and corners in the breed ring.

Working under command usually bolsters the confidence of dogs who are insecure around new people and strange dogs. Make the most of this phenomenon by practicing figure eights around people of all ages and around other trainers with steady dogs sitting at heel.

Equipment

Begin using two upright objects for posts. Place them eight feet apart and make sure they won't fall on your dog if bumped. For large dogs, place the posts twelve feet apart at first and work them back to eight feet as your dog achieves flexibility. Always use posts your dog can orient to—not rocks or spots drawn on the floor.

When your dog understands the exercise, substitute people for uprights at every opportunity.

TEACHING THE EXERCISE

Spend at least one week on each part before moving to the next.

Part One

Visualize your starting line. Most people find it easiest to start about two feet back from a spot exactly between the posts. Although you may go in either direction, most dogs do best if they begin with the left (inside) turn.

As you approach the starting line and your dog sees the posts, cue her by saying happily, "Eighter, let's do an eighter." Say it every time you prepare to begin the exercise, including in the show ring.

Stay about one and a half feet from the posts as you go around them, and use a taut lead to help your dog learn the rhythm of the exercise. Emphasize the change of pace by slowing slightly when your dog is on the inside turn and speeding up as you take your first step into the straightaway.

Part Two

Teach your dog to accelerate in preparation for the outside turn and keep up her speed around the outside by jumping into straightaways after circling the posts. Continue going slow around the inside post.

Part Three

Hold your lead with the normal amount of slack in it. Occasionally keep your pace steady as you will at the show, but continue to accentuate the changes of pace often while practicing.

Use distractions like people sitting and eating on the ground nearby and children playing with toys and balls. Offer your posts some cookies or chips and dip, but no napkins. Sometimes use children as posts—the show-giving club often does.

Correct bumping and forging on the inside turn by pivoting into your dog far enough so that you pass the post on your right side. Then do the "Jackie Gleason left turn" and halt. Run back to your starting point and begin again.

Correct wideness and lagging on the outside with a pivot so far to the right that you pass the post on your left side. Then jump ahead, release and start again. Always praise after every correction.

Never jump around a curve. The correction will not be properly directional and will be confusing and unfair.

Common Errors of the Dog and Simple Corrections

> *Bumping you on the inside turn.*
> *Lagging on the outside turn.*
> *Failing to change pace.* See "Teaching the Exercise" to correct these errors.
> *Failing to sit or poor sits.* If your dog does automatic sits correctly when heeling, a sit problem on the figure eight is due to lack of attention. She is probably distracted by the people/posts. Refer to sit corrections in "Heeling on Lead" (see page 61).

IN THE RING

Responsibility of the Dog

- Heel attentively.
- Perform changes of pace automatically to maintain heel position on inside and outside turns.
- Sit automatically when handler stops.

Responsibility of the Handler

- Continue at the same speed throughout the exercise.
- Keep a loose lead.
- Maintain an even radius around the posts.
- Maintain a natural posture.
- Maintain steady hands on the lead (no back and forth movement to cue speed).
- Give your dog enough space to maneuver around posts.
- Give commands in the same tone of voice you use when practicing.

Common Handler Errors and Simple Corrections

The first three listed in the section of "Heeling on Lead" also apply here.

> *Not maintaining an even radius around the posts.* Avoid the tendency to go too wide around the inside post. When you see others do this, it will look as if they are trying to walk around their dogs instead of the post. Slowing down and hugging the right post is a similar mistake. If you think you are making these errors, practice walking around the posts several times without your dog.

Taking a giant step upon entering the straightaway. A giant step will throw your dog off rhythm. Ask a friend to watch you.

Dipping your shoulders while circling. These turns are not so tight that you have to lean into them, but you may feel the urge all the same. Have a friend watch you.

Passing

If your dog is in heel position the majority of the time, remembers one of the sits, doesn't balk and is not fearful or aggressive toward the stewards (posts), she will probably pass. Make no corrections and just keep going, even if she is somewhere behind you on a tight lead, probably sniffing the steward. Chances are she will catch up when the judge says, "Halt." Chances are you will still pass the exercise. But if you slow down to wait for your dog, chances are you will fail.

Chew On This

Give your dog time to think her way through a new exercise before pushing for speed. Once they are confident, dogs often pick up the pace on their own.

Novice Stand for Examination

Prerequisites

Complete "Sneakaway Sessions" (see page 33) and the "Sitting for Examination" section of "Beginning Dual Training" (see page 45).

Begin work on the obedience stand at the same time as the sit and down-stays. Extremely wiggly dogs may need to gain some self-control by learning the sit-stay before the stand, but most dogs are better off learning the stand, sit and down around the same time.

What's New?

This is the first exercise your dog will perform off lead in the obedience ring. While the obedience examination is brief and doesn't include teeth and testicles, it takes confidence and concentration because you will be six feet away when the judge approaches your dog.

Your small dog's unabashed attitude on the table in the breed ring may not carry over to obedience. The table lets her meet the judge at waist level or higher, but in obedience she will be examined on the floor. Give her time to adjust. To understand how a stranger bending over her looks to a tiny dog, get down to her eye level and watch a friend approach and stand over you.

To understand how a stranger bending over her looks to a tiny dog, get down to her eye level and watch a friend approach and stand over you.

Relationship to Conformation

Did you ever see a dog look gorgeous outside the breed ring but develop cow hocks and a roached back when the judge approached to examine her? Or one that rocked backward and distorted her front, topline and rear? Conformation people refer to it as "falling apart," and it is usually caused by insecurity.

The obedience stand will help your dog be confident and happy in the conformation ring. An added bonus is that in the breed ring, if the style is "right" for your breed and your dog, you will be able to stack her, step to the end of your lead and allow the judge to examine her without any distraction from you. A pleasant presentation won't change your dog's conformation, but it sure looks impressive.

Equipment

Collar and lead.

TEACHING THE EXERCISE

Part One

Adjust your dog's collar and lead so that the attachment is centered on the front of your dog's neck. Place your right hand on the braided or stitched area of your lead and your knuckles on your dog's chest to prevent forward movement. Command "Staaand," run your left hand from her elbow to her tuck-up and gently lift her into a stand. She should step backward with her rear legs. Praise softly and keep your right hand on her chest, but remove your left hand. Be ready to touch her stifle if she tries to move her rear legs forward or sit. After a few seconds, release with a playful push on the chest and play. Practice ten times a day until your dog is relaxed about standing.

Part Two

Stand your dog as in part one, remove your hands from her chest and stifle, command and signal stay (described in "Steady She Stays—Introducing the Command," page 115) and stand next to her. If she tries to move or sit, correct with a soft horizontal lead jerk in the opposite direction of your dog's movement as you touch her stifle to prevent sitting.

When a dog is performing the stand, all lead corrections must be close and horizontal. Never jerk upward, down or from a distance because, in lead correction language, up means sit, down means down and a jerk from a distance means come.

With either hand on your dog's chest to prevent her from moving forward,

Placing your right hand against her chest will prevent your dog from moving forward while your left hand on the stifle stands her. Correct, if necessary, with a light, horizontal jerk at neck level and touch the stifle simultaneously.

If your dog moves as the examiner approaches, silently correct with a light horizontal jerk and touch her stifle to steady her.

begin circling her to your left and stroking her body with your free hand. Your dog will probably want to circle with you. Keep one hand on her chest as much as you can (this is not easy with short arms and a large dog) to correct turning, but don't say anything. Let your hands do all the talking.

If your dog moves her paws, don't try to put them back in place with your corrections. Simply try to prevent further movement. The more you fuss over paw movement, the worse your dog will fidget. Concentrate on correcting big mistakes because little movement mistakes usually disappear on their own later.

When you have walked all the way around your dog, step two feet in front of her for five seconds. If her head is down, tickle under her chin. Then walk all the way around her again to heel position. Praise, then push-play release. Sometimes circle again after praising to prevent anticipation and eventually remove your hand from her chest.

Part Three

Review "Sitting for Examination" from "Beginning Dual Training" and continue on when your dog is steady on the sit with strangers examining her and on the stand with you examining her.

Ask someone your dog knows to play judge and instruct them not to talk or make eye contact, but smoothly, calmly and quickly show your dog their hand, touch her head, back and rump and walk away. Talking and eye contact will make a fearful dog more paranoid and an outgoing one too social. Stand your dog and go about two feet in front of her. Give no verbal corrections as the "judge" approaches or examines her because she could misinterpret them and believe she is being corrected for allowing a person to touch her. If she moves, silently walk in and use the horizontal jerk to correct and the stifle touch to steady her. Then leave quickly and let the examiner try again. Whenever your dog makes a mistake twice, return to the sit for examination to correct her.

The stand-stay is often the easiest exercise for a dog to learn, but serious problems like submitting into a sit, constantly fidgeting or refusing to accept examination may take considerable time to correct. Keep calm and correct swiftly and with minimal fussing.

As your dog becomes steady, be certain you are not touching her when you command "Stay." Leave with your back to her and turn to face her from six feet away. When returning around her to heel position, sometimes circle twice or continue back out in front of her. Always release the stand with a push-play. Off-lead practice should wait until your dog has learned the heel free. Then do the stand a few times with your lead lying on the ground before removing it.

Common Errors of the Dog and Simple Corrections

> *Moving away or sitting before or during examination.* This is a stay problem. The horizontal stand correction must always be given lightly or it

can pull your dog out of position, so go back to the sit for examination where you can give sharper corrections. Remain close while your dog is being examined and correct movement with a lead correction, not your voice. After your dog succeeds several times in a row with the same examiner, try it from a stand. Return to the sit for examination whenever your dog makes two mistakes in a row on the stand.

Sitting as the handler returns without waiting to be released. She is anticipating, and it is probably your fault. Your dog has probably been good at this exercise so often that you have started taking it for granted. Now she has memorized the pattern. Knowing you will release her when you return, she simply saves you the trouble.

Use horizontal lead corrections and the stifle touch to correct and be creative with your returns. Sometimes walk around her in the other direction. Other times get halfway around and "discover" something on the ground that you must examine. Often circle her twice or circle, go back out a few feet and return again.

Growling or snapping. This book is meant for people who show in conformation as well as obedience, and breed ring dogs should be broodstock quality. Dogs of such poor temperament that they growl or snap at the examiner should never be used for breeding, and their problems are not dealt with here.

IN THE RING

Responsibility of the Dog

- Remain standing in place until released.
- Accept the judge's examination without shyness or resentment.

Responsibility of the Handler

- If you manually guide your dog by the collar after giving up your lead, do it gently.
- Be sure your dog is in a comfortable position before giving the stay command.
- Do not give the stay command until you are standing beside your dog in heel position without touching her.
- Step off on your right foot when leaving your dog so she won't confuse it with heeling.
- Learn how far six feet in front of you is and go that far, but no farther.
- When returning to your dog, go all the way to heel position.

Common Handler Errors and Simple Corrections

Placing a faulty dog in a hard-to-hold show pose instead of in her natural position. If your dog is cow-hocked and you stack her rear straight, as you will in the breed ring, she will probably move her back legs when you walk away. A poor rear won't be penalized in obedience, but moving will.

- *Glancing back at your dog as you leave her, or backing away.*

- *Not returning all the way to heel position.* Honest, this is a common error. After spending weeks teaching a dog to find heel position, handlers can't find it themselves and lose points for returning to their dog's rump instead of her shoulder.

Passing

If your dog remains where you left her until the examination is over, she should pass. Moving her paws slightly loses points but doesn't make her fail. Moving a little or sitting before you get back, but after the examination is over, also loses points. If she shows any aggression or extreme shyness, she will fail.

Most dog and handler teams earn full credit for this exercise. Since everything you need to know to earn a perfect score has already been included, this section has no "blue" counterpart.

Sky Hooked

OUR SKY HOOKS, commonly known as throw chains, differ from the norm because they are flying objects that don't warn with a jingle. Just when your dog thinks about taking off on her own, these silent missiles seem to drop from the sky and mentally hook her to the safety of staying with you.

Your dog must never see you throw a sky hook, because she is supposed to think it is a warning from "up there" not to run away from you.

Since you will throw the hook at your dog's rump, its size and weight must relate to the size of your dog. Make your sky hooks out of either one-eighth-ounce, one-quarter-ounce or one-half-ounce egg-shaped fishing weights (sinkers) strung on ten- to twenty-pound test monofilament (fishing line) and tied in the shape of a bracelet. They are inexpensive, have no sharp edges and can be weighted to surprise, but not hurt, any dog. A one-ounce bracelet (composed of eight one-eighth-ounce sinkers) would be good for a three-pound Chihuahua. A six-ounce bracelet (twelve one-half-ounce sinkers) works on dogs of around twenty-five pounds, and you can figure up or down from there with eight ounces as the upper limit. Paint your sinkers white or yellow if they are too hard to relocate after using them in grass. Unlike more cumbersome and sometimes tattletale chains, sky hooks are nearly silent and take up less space, so you can carry several hooks in your pocket at a time without jingling, and collect them when the training session is over.

Directions for using sky hooks will be included in the "Teaching the Exercise" section whenever they are suggested as teaching aids. The following guidelines for their use hold true in every case.

Sky Hook Guidelines

- Always wait until your dog is looking elsewhere before throwing a sky hook.
- When your dog approaches a distracting situation, have a hook ready in your hand before you call her.
- Throw fast. If you lob the hook slowly, your dog could turn and see you throw or get hit on the head instead of the rump.
- Throw only when landing on the mark is a sure thing.
- Keep your dog on lead when using hooks until she realizes that she should return to you.
- Throw the hook at yourself (or let a family member toss one at you) before trying it on your dog. When you know what it feels like, you'll understand that your dog is reacting to surprise, not pain.
- Never let your dog see you pick up and pocket the hooks.

Novice and Open Heel Free and Open Figure Eight

Prerequisites

When your dog heels attentively amid distractions and will heel cold on the first command with no tension on the lead, she is ready to learn the heel free.

What's New?

You will have to repeat, off lead, the same Novice heeling pattern you performed on lead.

The Open pattern may differ from the one you became used to in Novice, and patterns often vary from judge to judge, so arrive early enough to watch a few dogs work before your turn. If you are the first entry in your class, the judge will explain the pattern.

The off-lead figure eight will not be included in the Novice pattern but is required in Open.

Relationship to Conformation

The ability to work as a team "without strings attached" increases rapport, trust and mutual awareness. It also makes the breed ring feel tame by comparison, so you will lose your stage fright and be able to concentrate on your handling.

Equipment

Besides your regular collar and lead, attach the tab during practice from now on. You will also need a light line and sky hooks. (See "Collars, Leads, Lines and Corrections," page 25, and "Sky Hooked," page 93.)

TEACHING THE EXERCISE

Does your dog really understand heel position or did she just become adept at following the lead? No, don't remove it to find out. Instead, hold it in your right hand, behind your back, for a few minutes of heeling a day. She can hardly follow it if it is no longer in front of her.

The object of this test is to see if your dog will right her own errors. Continue going the opposite way whenever your dog deviates from heel position, but don't take a large enough step to jerk the lead and correct her. Except that the lead is behind your back, your movements will be the same as for heeling on lead, just smaller and gentler. Go left if your dog forges or crowds you. If she lags, sniffs or is inattentive, jump straight ahead and make a quick right and then a little jump for wideness. If your lead tightens often, your dog was probably following it instead of heeling, at least part of the time.

To remind your dog to watch you instead of the lead, keep the lead behind your back but grab it with your left hand, place your left hand on your left thigh and jump ahead so it jerks the same as it did when it was in front of your legs. Praise after correcting, keep walking and remove your left hand from the lead. Try circles, turns and changes of pace. If your dog tries to cross behind you to the wrong side, place your left hand back on the lead, press it against your left thigh and jump ahead again.

Frequent mistakes with the lead behind your back mean that your dog needs more heeling work with the lead in front. Limit "behind your back" practice to only a few good minutes per session until her heeling improves.

Introducing the Sky Hooks

The same week you introduce your dog to heeling with the lead behind your back, have the sky hooks ready. They work especially well on potential runaways. Begin by reviewing "Sky Hook Guidelines" (see page 94).

Hold the lead in front of you in your right hand and a sky hook in your left. Don't toss the hook unless your dog forges. When she does, if you are sure she is no longer watching you, throw the hook at her rump, do an about-turn, jump forward and praise your amazed dog as soon as she gets back to your side. Create

Preparing for off-lead heeling. The lead should be held slack behind your back unless you are correcting. Take a small jump ahead if your dog lags or goes wide.

Lead behind back. To correct, grab the lead with your left hand and jump with your left knuckles on your thigh.

If your dog lags on the light line, jump ahead to give her a chance to recover.

If she continues lagging, turn around and walk up to the tab.

Quickly wrap the line around your hand and run with it on your hip. Arrange it so that your dog has no slack unless she is in heel position.

distractions, repeat the toss whenever you can make the opportunity arise and always behave as if nothing unusual has happened.

Use the sky hooks only for forging and correct other errors with the same turns and jumps you already learned. When your dog learns to come back to you as soon as a sky hook hits and performs well with the lead behind your back, you are ready for the first step of off-lead heeling.

Introducing the Tab and Light Line

Attach the light line to your dog's tab and let it drag on the ground. Heel a few minutes with the lead behind your back. When you remove it, command "Mancha, heel," and move out confidently and quickly. If your dog doesn't move with you or meanders, goes wide or lags, immediately do the opposite of what was on her agenda. Jump ahead or to the right for sniffing, lagging, wideness or inattention. Change to a slow pace for forging. Turn left when she is crowding or if she is looking at you while only forging slightly. When your dog returns to heel position, give verbal praise. If she does not correct her position, walk (don't run) up to the tab, slide your left hand down the line to about eighteen inches from the collar (more for a small dog and less for a large one), and wind the line around your hand a few times so it won't slide. Run with it on your left hip. When your dog catches up and resumes heel position, praise her verbally, continue walking and drop the line.

Hooking Runaways

Some dogs try to run away when you approach to grab the tab, and others cavort away when they realize the lead is gone. A sky hook in your best throwing hand will keep you ready for either possibility. The instant your dog tries to leave for any reason, throw the hook at her rump, step on the line so she can't get away, walk up to her matter-of-factly and grab the tab. Slide your left hand down the line to correct as explained above.

Off Lead Guidelines

- Always grab the tab rather than the line. If you grab for the line, it will probably be tangled around your dog's legs, making a good correction impossible. Ultimately, you will wean your dog off the light line so she might as well learn from the start that she can't run away from an off-lead correction.
- Gradually become more demanding and give your dog less opportunity to fix her own mistakes before you make a correction.
- Work on a lot of turns and changes of pace with your lead behind your back and repeat them later on the light line. That way you will learn if

your dog is just walking with you, following the lead or actually heeling.

- Around difficult distractions, practice on lead with the lead in front so you will achieve quicker corrections.
- If you have several problems, put your dog back on lead to work them out. Mistakes magnify off lead and staying on lead longer often saves time in the long run.
- When your dog can work cold around distractions on line, shorten (cut) the line by 20 percent of its length every few days.
- When you get down to only the tab, use the following off-lead corrections:
  —If your dog lags, stop immediately. Walk to the tab and give it a jerk as you continue walking.
  —Correct wideness by stopping, walking to the tab and sidestepping right. Use your left hand on the outside of your dog's left rear leg to tuck her into a sit next to you.
  —Use the "Jackie Gleason left turn" (see "Heeling on Lead," page 73) to correct forging and crowding.
  —Correct no sits and crooked sits the same as you would on lead.

Common Errors of the Dog and Simple Corrections

Identical to those described in "Heeling on Lead" and "Novice Figure Eight," but in addition:

- Leaving you and going off exploring on her own.
- Leaving the ring.
- Stopping and watching you walk the pattern alone.

If your dog persists in repeating the same error, the fastest way to correct it is to work the problem out on lead. Runaway problems on dogs who heel well on lead should be corrected on line with sky hooks.

IN THE RING

Responsibility of the Dog

Identical to "Heeling on Lead" and "Novice Figure Eight."

Responsibility of the Handler

Identical to "Heeling on Lead" and "Novice Figure Eight" except that items referring to the lead itself do not apply. In addition:

- Read your dog. If she is about to race from the ring, kiss the judge or bury her nose in the steward's pocket, give a second command to heel.

Identical to "Heeling on Lead" and "Novice Figure Eight" except the item about the tight lead does not apply.

Passing

If your dog is in heel position more often than not, remembers at least one sit (although dogs who heeled but never remembered to sit have qualified), receives no more than one extra command to heel and doesn't try to leave the ring, she will probably pass. Identical "iffy" performances could pass under one judge and fail under another.

101

Reel in as you back up and praise.

Recall

Prerequisites

When your dog can do a solid, off-lead sit-stay (see "Steady She Stays," page 115) and knows what "come" means, she is ready to begin. When you can give the stay command once and walk away without backing up or sneaking a look over your shoulder, *you* are ready.

Review "On Lead Outdoors," from "Conditioning Carefree Comes" (see page 17), and try it when your dog is walking leisurely on a loose lead, not at heel. Using your dog's name and the command "Come," practice it several times over a three-day period, with lively praise.

What's New?

Your dog will do a sit-stay while you walk to the other side of the ring (about thirty-five feet). Although brief, this lonesome stay could make your dog more insecure than during the Group stays. With no line of dogs to remind her which exercise she is performing, if she loses concentration she may think she should have heeled off with you.

Your dog must come when you call and end up close enough so that you could touch her head without moving your feet or stretching your arms. Ideally she should be facing you and sitting straight with her body centered in front of, but not touching, your feet. Truth is, if she jumps up and licks you before sitting on your toes, she will still pass.

This exercise ends with a finish, which means your dog should return to heel position on command with no assistance from you. An occasional dog becomes very confused when learning to finish and takes longer to learn that portion of this exercise than all the other Novice exercises combined. If your dog is reliable on all the other exercises and you are in a hurry to put a CD on her, you can qualify with a dog that never learned to finish, provided you don't care about your score. When the judge says, "Finish," say your dog's name and "Heel," and look disappointed when nothing happens. You will lose points for no finish but not enough to fail the exercise.

Relationship to Conformation

Reinforces the stay command.

Equipment

Besides your collar and lead, you will need your lines, tab and sky hooks.

TEACHING THE EXERCISE

Until now, when you wanted your dog near, you called "Come." In her mind "come" meant somewhere close to you—beside you, just in front of or behind you.

When teaching the recall, use the command "Front." In your dog's mind "front" will become a position. It means sitting straight in front of you, facing you.

Teaching the Position

Begin teaching fronts from two different starting points and mix them up. Sometimes call your dog front while practicing heeling and other times while out for a casual walk. In either case command "Mancha, front," and immediately back up, reel in the lead and praise. Continue reeling and backing until you have a grip on the lead close enough to the collar so that you can control your dog's front end while your left hand guides your dog's rear into a straight sit.

After a week of automatically reeling and guiding, test your dog's response. When she is on lead doing her own thing, stand still and call her to front. If she doesn't respond right away, give a quick, horizontal jerk toward you with an immediate release. With a large dog, back up as you jerk, but still release immediately. Keep slack in your lead instead of reeling her in, but when she arrives, guide her into a sit and praise her.

Continue practicing on lead and test occasionally until your dog's front suits you and she can do it without your guidance or movement.

Longe Line Time

Remove the lead, attach the longe line and practice fronts just as you did on lead, including the occasional test. Hold the longe line for the first few sessions, then drop it and step on it before calling your dog front. Correct by picking it up and jerking (quickly, horizontally toward you) until your dog corrects herself too quickly for you to be effective. Then use off-lead corrections instead. Walk up to the tab, give a horizontal jerk and praise as you back up and remove your hand from the tab. You will use the same correction when your dog actually is off lead and line.

More Hooking Runaways

Bring on the distractions. People opening and closing car doors and gates, cheering and clapping, treats on the ground and other animals are all fair, but never personalize a distraction by having someone call your dog by name.

When she tries to cut classes heeling on lead, your dog knows she sets off corrections from above. Now it is time to show her that recall failures also launch missiles and the safest place to be is sitting in front of you receiving praise.

If some distractions make your dog ignore you, get those sky hooks ready. Put her on lead and use your imagination to create a fascinating distraction. When she is engrossed in it, get directly behind her so that she cannot see you from the corner of her eye, and give your front command. If she doesn't look at you, bounce the hook off her rump, quickly reel her into a front and praise lavishly. Soon she will decide that it is better to obey you and be praised than to ignore you and risk a butt beaning.

The sky hooks also work on dogs who try to run away from an off-lead correction (see "Hooking Runaways," page 99). After you stop your dog, give a horizontal jerk tab correction, run backward and praise as she fronts. If you have a constant runaway problem, put your dog on a fifty-foot light line so that it will be impossible to miss when you have to step on it. Then walk on it all the way to the tab and use the tab to make your correction. As your dog becomes reliable, cut the line down. You can remove 20 percent of its length every third day if you have tested your dog around tough new distractions and she has done well.

Adding the Beginning

When stays are solid and inattention and runaway problems have been dealt with, put the first two parts of the recall exercise together sometimes. With your dog on a sit-stay on lead, walk forward confidently and turn to face her. Don't call her every time. Sometimes return around her to heel position, other times look busy tying your shoe or examining a nearby tree. Call your dog about one-third of the time, sometimes after several seconds of busywork. When you

To teach the finish, step back with your right leg and guide your dog behind your left leg. A blockade creates an alley for your dog to go through and allows her to walk easily into a straight sit.

do call, sometimes remain in place as she fronts and other times promote a speedy recall by backing up.

If your dog does not come from the sit when you call her, give an abrupt horizontal lead jerk and run backward.

When your dog responds well on lead, change to the light line and tab and have your sky hooks ready. Begin increasing the distance you leave your dog. When you are pleased with her response, stretch the light line out on the ground between you so you can easily step on it if you need to.

If your dog fails to respond, or becomes distracted on her way in, calmly walk up to her, grab the tab and make your horizontal correction as you move backward to the place where you called her. Should she turn to run from you, stop her with a sky hook and reel her in as you run backward and praise.

Cut the line down gradually, using the same formula as before.

The Finish

Step One: Set up a barrier on your left side, to make a path just wide enough for your dog to walk through. Standing beside a wall is easiest, but a sofa, table or car will do fine.

Start with your dog in front position, command "Side," and, using a short grip on the lead, pull your dog through the alley. If she is difficult to pull, step back with your right leg, leaving your left leg stationary so that your dog learns to go behind it. After she is through the alley, let your dog turn around to her left and walk back to sit in heel position. Praise profusely.

Step Two: When your dog goes through the alley easily, give the command and signal toward the alley with a sweeping gesture of your left arm. If your dog doesn't move, use a horizontal jerk to get her going.

Step Three: When your dog finishes on command, remove the alley. Use a jerk if she ignores the command. If she tries to turn short, guide her behind your leg with a tight lead. Correct sits as described in "Heeling on Lead" (see page 73). As she becomes proficient, sometimes give the verbal command alone and sometimes use the signal alone, but don't use them together anymore.

All Together Now

Once your dog has learned the finish, the pieces of the recall exercise may be put together and the distance gradually extended until she is reliable at fifty feet. Practice at various distances, on lead or line and off. Vary the exercise by using different distractions. Return to your dog frequently instead of calling her and sometimes run away from her after you call and hug her when she catches you instead of doing a formal front. Alternate releasing your dog from front position, circling her while she is sitting front, and command the finish.

Common Errors of the Dog and Simple Corrections

> *Breaking the stay* (following you, anticipating the recall, standing, down-ing or moving out of position). This is a stay problem, not a recall problem. Move quickly to grab the tab or lead and swing her back in exactly the direction she came. When she is back where she was, correct with an upward jerk. Review "Steady She Stays" (see page 115).
>
> *Not coming, leaving the ring, slow response, sniffing or playing.* Walk to the tab and give a horizontal jerk toward you. Take your hand off the tab, back up until you are where you were when you called and praise. If your dog detours on the way, repeat the tab correction until she commits to doing the front without your hand on the tab. If this is difficult, you took her off lead too soon. Give her a couple more weeks on line, with distractions.
>
> *No or poor front.* To guide your dog into a good front, pull the tab as you back up and praise and position your dog's rear with your free hand.

IN THE RING

Responsibility of the Dog

- Remain in a sit-stay while you walk to the other end of the ring.
- Come immediately when called.
- Sit in front facing you.
- Go to heel position on command.

Responsibility of the Handler

- Give clear, audible commands, using the same tone and posture used during practice. If you are normally cheerful, a gruff command could upset your dog.
- Leave your dog confidently, without looking back over your shoulder.
- Keep your hands at your sides.
- Do not use body English.

Common Handler Errors and Simple Corrections

Adopting a stiff, unnatural stance. Notice where you place your feet at practice. At the show, a case of nerves could make you stand with your anklebones banging together, when your dog is used to seeing your feet a few inches apart. Your dog is aiming her "front" at your legs, so give her the view she is used to.

Issuing double commands. Beware of leaning forward when calling your dog, bending your knees as she comes or flipping your fingers in the direction of the finish.

Passing

If your dog stays until you call her, responds to a single command and comes and stays close enough so that you could easily touch her, she will probably pass.

Learn to pet your dog on her right side when she is sitting at heel. Petting on the left encourages leaning and crooked sits.

The Brittany, Ch. Three B's Ham It Up, CDX, owned, bred, trained and handled by Jan Hall. Brittanies generally have a good aptitude for training and many have achieved noteworthy success in conformation, obedience and, of course, as gun dogs.

Chew On This

The faster you go, the slower you get there.

An Ounce of Prevention

IT TAKES A LOT LONGER to fix problems than to teach exercises properly in the first place. Failures are time-consuming and expensive because as long as your dog is entered in shows, you have to keep practicing, and the more she fails, the more shows you have to enter.

Applying the following principles to your training program will dramatically increase your dog's learning rate and comprehension:

- Break each exercise into small, easy components. For example, the down-stay is easy if you postpone teaching it until your dog has mastered the down command and the sit-stay.
- Increase the difficulty of the tasks gradually and only after simpler tasks have been mastered.
- Always have a game plan ready for dealing with mistakes before you need to use it.
- Never be reluctant to backtrack if learning grinds to a halt.
- Regard mistakes as a positive, necessary learning experience for your dog.
- Repeatedly test with distractions at each level.

PROOF POSITIVE

The more their dog does a perfect high jump in practice, the more confident some trainers feel about her ability to perform that exercise at a show. Unfortunately, if that dog is never tested, but performs the exercise week after week in the trainer's backyard, the distractions at the show will turn the retrieve over the jump into an entirely different exercise from the dog's perspective.

By proofing your dog, you will avoid the hold-your-breath, cross-your-fingers method of training.

Litter the Learning Process with Mistakes

Training with distractions uncovers weaknesses and enables you to eliminate them before they become problems. Taking your dog into the show ring without distraction-proofing her first is like walking around patches of thin ice to get to the middle of the lake; while sidestepping you risk falling in at the deepest point.

Distractions

A distraction is anything your dog is interested in. Birds, food and children fascinate most dogs and therefore make good distractions. Seek out or invent distractions to practice around during every training session. Hire a helper or schedule training for when the kids come home from school. Practice in the evening when the neighbor walks his dog, or drive to a park or a friend's kennel.

When your dog becomes obsessed with a distraction, don't give commands or hold her back. The more you restrain, the more she will believe the distraction is desirable, so she will struggle harder to free herself.

Tune your dog in by doing sneakaways (see "Sneakaway Sessions," page 33) in the presence of the exciting distraction until she stays by your side on a loose lead. Gradually progress to practicing stays, recalls and heeling near the fascinating distraction. Even advanced dogs must learn to do the basics around distractions before they can concentrate on more complicated tasks, so take note of the type of distractions your dog becomes obsessed with during Novice training and seek them out later when working on Open and Utility.

Setups

Setups are planned events where you expect your dog to make a mistake and are physically and mentally prepared to correct her. If you need to correct inattention on the recall, you might ask a friend to run a dog alongside yours after you called. If you need to strengthen the signal exercise, you might plan to have someone open a door behind your dog just as you are giving the signal.

Setups will correct problems only if your dog has no opportunity to practice the bad behavior in between. You always have to be prepared and able to correct. That means pulling your dog from events where you can't correct her (shows, sanctioned matches and demonstrations) until she no longer falls for setups no matter how creative or tempting.

MAKE TRAINING EASY—NOT SIMPLE

A chef must carefully combine the ingredients in a recipe to create a culinary masterpiece. Even a pizza is made by preparing a crust, then layering the toppings in a particular sequence. Stirring together the flour, tomato sauce, cheese and meat, then tossing it in the oven, won't make a dish that tastes like a pizza even though it has the same ingredients. Dog training also requires you to cover preliminary steps and follow a logical sequence.

It may seem simpler and faster to forgo the sneakaway sessions and jump right into command training. But until your dog maintains attention around distractions, she will learn commands but will only perform them well in your backyard. A familiar lament of nonqualifiers is "But she always does it right at home."

Remain close to your dog during the learning phase of an exercise. The recall will eventually be done from forty feet away, but begin teaching from one step in front. That enables you to easily maneuver and guide your dog and gives her a chance to experience success quickly. As her confidence increases, so can your distances.

Who's Afraid of the Big Bad Distraction?

Anxiety-producing distractions, like noisy vacuum cleaners or someone dragging a metal garbage can, can be especially useful for building confidence. Insisting that your dog concentrate on her job will eventually diminish her fear, and gaining the ability to work around a scary object is the canine version of overcoming anxiety.

Introduce fear-inducing distractions after your dog has a basic understanding of an exercise, and be prepared to deal with her worst possible reaction. Begin with your dog on lead on a sit-stay. Stand one step away and don't talk to her or you may telegraph your own apprehension and reinforce her fearfulness. Act confident and correct abruptly, as if to say, "There is *nothing* strange about this situation."

If a distraction makes your dog so panic-stricken that you cannot control her, think of a way to temporarily tone it down until she can maintain attention on you. Later bring the distraction closer and gradually intensify it as your dog becomes steady on the sit-stay. If it is a noise, make it louder. If it is an object or animal, move it around more. The process may take several weeks. When your dog will hold a sit-stay with the distraction close and you a greater distance away, begin using it on heeling and the recall.

Distraction-proofing Your Super Showman

It is especially important that your breed dog tune you in when it is her turn to bait, stack and gait. She won't become preoccupied with another handler opening his bait bag, applause, a flapping tent or a rambunctious pup if you use these types of distractions in practice.

Taboo: Many conformation judges expect dogs to bait for them. Therefore, don't set up situations where someone distracts your dog by approaching from the front, making eye contact, talking and presenting food or a toy and then correct her for responding. Directly inviting your dog, then correcting her for accepting, will hurt her showmanship and may teach her not to bait for others.

Back Up to Leap Forward

No matter how long your dog has performed an exercise well, some day she may start messing it up. Swift as you may be to correct her, sometimes the only solution is to remember how you taught the exercise and backtrack to a level where she is successful. When you believe she understands what you expect and knows you will see to it that she does it properly, gradually increase the difficulty.

Don't be tempted to move ahead when your dog "only needs a little help." Wait until she is doing it herself. Suppose you are accompanying your retrieve command with an arm gesture and plan to slowly wean your dog off the cue as you throw the dumbbell farther. Unfortunately, your dog will become more dependent on that cue the longer you use it and the farther you toss the dumbbell. The dog who retrieves a dumbbell placed three feet in front of her without a gesture is closer to "ring ready" than a dog who retrieves a dumbbell thrown one hundred feet with a gesture. Waiting to advance until your dog can do small steps all by herself will always speed your progress.

Chew On This

One practice in a strange place is more useful than five sessions at home. Strange places don't have to be far away. The next block, a friend's yard and the grocery-store parking lot are all new to your dog.

Steady She Stays

Prerequisites

Review "The Sit" and "Standing Pretty" from "Beginning Dual Training" (see pages 46 and 53).

When your dog will sit for fifteen seconds and stand for ten under the steadying influence of your hands, remain in position while being praised and understands release, she is ready to start the stay.

When you have learned to give the sit or stand command only once and use your hands to elicit compliance, *you* are ready.

What's New?

You and your dog will line up and walk into the ring with several other dogs and handlers. When everyone is evenly spaced, side by side, to the judge's satisfaction, you will remove your armband and lead and place them behind your dog with the number on the armband showing. Even though your dog is probably already sitting, you will be told to "Sit your dogs." On the command "Leave your dogs," you are permitted to say "Stay" and give the hand signal. Then you will walk to the other side of the ring with the rest of the handlers, turn and face your dog. After one minute, the judge will say, "Back to your dogs." You will return to heel position by walking around the back of your dog, who must remain in place until the judge says, "Exercise finished." Then you may release her or softly praise her, whichever works best for you.

Soon the judge will say, "Are you ready?" and will expect your dog to be sitting in heel position. When everyone is ready, the judge will command, "Down your dogs," and you are allowed a verbal command and a hand signal. When the dogs are down and facing forward, the judge will say, "Leave your dog," and handlers will cross the ring again. This time your dog must remain in position for the longest three minutes of your life. When time is up, you will be told to "Return to your dogs," and handlers will walk around their dogs to heel position. Again, your dog must stay in place until the judge says, "Exercise finished."

Relationship to Conformation

This exercise teaches your dog to concentrate on what she is doing and not become distracted by other dogs and handlers. It also reinforces the stay command.

Equipment

Your dog will enter the ring wearing her collar and lead, and you will wear your armband. Before the exercise begins, you will unsnap your dog's lead and place it, along with your armband, behind your dog. If you are outdoors, adjust your equipment so that your lead keeps your armband from blowing away and your armband number is visible.

During training, you will need your regular collar and lead, a fifty-foot light line and a watch to time your stays. A ten-second stay takes longer than you might guesstimate.

TEACHING THE EXERCISE

Begin by reviewing the sit and down as taught in "Beginning Dual Training." On medium to large dogs, use an upward jerk (two-handed, if necessary) to correct the sit and a downward jerk to correct the down. For small dogs, put just enough force in your corrections to be effective. You may also have to push your dog's rump during the sit and her shoulder during the down. These are corrections, so don't use them unless you have already taught your dog the meaning of the commands and she is balking at performing them. If you trained on the table, make the transition to the floor by practicing sits and downs for a few days before using the stay command.

Introducing the Command and Signal

When your dog responds to the commands, begin the sit-stay on lead. Command "Stay," firmly but no louder than your ordinary speaking voice. Say

Correct movement by stepping in front of your dog and applying an upward jerk.

Keep tension on the lead as you act busy.

117

it only once and make it a longer word than "Sit" but not as long as "Staaand."

To give the hand signal, swing your left arm, palm facing the rear, straight out to the left. Then return your arm to a natural position at your side. Your dog should see your palm hesitate for an instant a few inches from her nose, so adjust your arm position accordingly. Give the command and signal simultaneously. Stand beside your dog, use low-key verbal and sometimes physical praise, and be ready to correct if necessary. Gradually increase the stay to twenty seconds and release with push-play.

One Step at a Time

When your dog stays twenty seconds with you beside her, try stepping in front of and facing her. Always step off on your right foot and leave a little slack in your lead. Pay attention and be ready to correct. If you are lucky, seeing you move will entice her to forget she is on command and move with you. That gives you an opportunity to reinforce her stays. Dogs learn by making mistakes and being corrected for them, so don't let her down by allowing your mind to wander. When moving away from your dog after giving a stay command, always step off on your right foot.

Don't say anything if your dog moves before you get in front of her. Just reposition her with a jerk on the collar and only slight pressure on her rear. If she moves after you are facing her, jerk upward abruptly on the lead to make her sit. If that isn't enough, reach over and place your left hand on her rear. When she is steady, act busy. Check out your shoe. Examine a pebble. Try the sit-stay in several different places so you can inventory the refrigerator, talk on the phone and sit in a chair. Actually, you will be watching your dog every second because if she moves, you should slide your hand down the lead instantly to give the upward jerk. To be effective, the correction must be immediate and silent.

Return to your dog frequently to praise her. When you step away again, be ready to correct if she tries to follow you. Sometimes, when you are in front of her, put slight horizontal tension on the lead. When she understands the stay she will brace against the pull to remain in place. If she doesn't, correct.

Use tempting distractions and release your dog with much praise after she has held steady for fifteen or twenty seconds. If she gives in to the distractions, correct silently and quickly. Gradually increase the time to thirty seconds and extend the distance, one step at a time. Remain alert to movement and correct by stepping in close before jerking upward.

Going Full Circle

When your dog stays for thirty seconds with you three feet in front of her, she is ready to learn the return you will do in the ring. To return to your dog after facing her, walk all the way past her left side and around her back to heel position. If she moves, say nothing, but reposition her where she was with an

118

upward, slightly backward jerk of the lead, and start over. Be careful not to step on her tail, but as she becomes steady, sometimes touch her side or leg gently with the side of your foot as you walk around her. One day she may be crowded in the ring, and if she is used to you returning close, brushing against her during competition won't upset her.

Practice until your dog remains steady at the sit-stay for three minutes, with distractions (people, pets, goodies on the ground nearby), with you a lead length away. Vary by sometimes walking around her twice. Also stop at various angles behind her, then go back out front instead of returning to heel. If she moves, no matter how little, give a silent, abrupt lead correction.

It's Post Time

Tying your dog to a post or tree is the best way to begin increasing your distance from her. The post should be behind her, and she should be facing away from it. Put her on sit-stay first, then fasten her to it. In the ring, when you have to place your armband and lead behind her, she will be used to you going behind her before you leave her. With luck she may even imagine that you are tying her to something.

Little by little, move farther away. If your dog moves, go back and correct her silently. You won't have to worry about her running off to avoid a correction, because she is tied. Be creative in your use of distractions. Noise and other people calling commands such as "Down" and "Come" should be included, but no one should call your dog by name or direct a command at her.

On the Line

When your dog does well tied, put her on a fifty-foot light line attached to a tab and let it lie loose on the ground between you and her. Invent new distractions and run in to correct her when she moves (if she is the type that melts, walk in). When she no longer tries to dodge corrections, begin cutting the line as described in the recall exercise.

The Down-Stay

To teach the down-stay, repeat these lessons in order with new distractions, substituting the "down-stay" for "sit-stay" and "downward jerk" on the lead for "upward jerk."

General Rules for Sit- and Down-Stays (Novice or Open)

- Correct silently. The more you repeat commands, the more your dog learns to ignore them. If your dog didn't listen the first time, let your hands and lead do the talking.

With your dog tied to a stationary object, increase distance and use creative distractions.

When teaching the out-of-sight stay, hide around a corner with your dog on lead so that you can correct quickly. Proof by throwing distractions from around the corner.

Never yell 'Quiet' unless you are able to correct...

- Pay attention. Move in for corrections the instant your dog moves or she won't know what the correction was for.
- Leave immediately after a lead correction.
- The strength of your correction should relate to your dog's size, her level of training, why she moved and how excited or distracted she is. When a correction is ineffective, it should be strengthened.
- When returning to your dog, occasionally crowd her, brush against her lightly or step over her.
- Practice stays in as many different places as you can.

Out-of-Sight Open Stays

In the Open ring, dogs must do a sit-stay for three minutes with handlers out of sight and a down-stay with handlers out of sight for five minutes. You will enter the ring and prepare your dog just as in Novice, but when the judge says, "Leave your dogs," a steward leads everyone to a location away from the ring where they indulge in group worry until the steward leads them back.

Teaching Open Stays

Find a corner, such as the corner of your house or kennel. Place your dog on one side, command "Stay" and walk around the corner. Hold the lead and toss out distractions such as treats or balls. Use a tiny mirror or a spy to tell you what your dog is doing. Return immediately and silently to correct for any movement.

When your dog is steady around the corner, leave her in other areas—first on a light line, and later off line entirely. Watch her the entire time from a window in the house, from under the car or from behind the high jump (make a tiny gap by placing a pen between the boards). Try this in different locations and create tempting new distractions. Return quickly when correction is needed.

Common Errors of the Dog and Simple Corrections

Sniffing, eating grass, playing. Down your dog in an area where there are many interesting scents from dogs, food or other animals and correct with an abrupt cuff under the chin as soon as she lowers her head to sniff. When she no longer tries to sniff when going down, practice the sit- and down-stay with aromatic distractions, like empty tuna fish cans or a cookie on the ground a few feet from her. Correct your dog if her nose makes contact with the ground, another dog or any surface. The sniffing correction will usually correct air scenting too, but if it doesn't use a cuff under the chin or a downward jerk on the lead when your dog stretches her neck to air scent.

121

Staring at the dog beside her. Staring can lead to a scuffle and between the embarrassment and the veterinarian bill, it will ruin your day. Go back to practicing sneakaways around other dogs until your dog no longer is engrossed by her neighbors.

Whining or barking. First teach your dog to be quiet on command in the house or the kennel. Learning to quiet down on command will not deter her from being a watchdog any more than learning the down-stay will turn her into a couch potato.

Command ''Quiet,'' and simultaneously shake your dog by the scruff of her neck or swat her under the chin. After you have done this half a dozen times, give her the opportunity to become quiet on command before being corrected. Never yell ''Quiet'' unless you are able to correct, so if your dog is barking by a window and you just stepped out of the tub, say nothing until you have your clothes on. Once you give the command, always follow through with corrections if needed, even though your dog may not be barking at the actual instant that you reach her to correct. Use the same command and correction when she is noisy on the stays.

If your dog only makes noise when you are far away during the stays, attach a line and have someone hold it behind her. When she makes noise, they should jerk her off-balance. Then you return and give the correction for moving off the stay.

If your dog whines and barks because she is hyper, use sneakaways (see ''Sneakaway Sessions,'' page 33) to tone down her excitability and make her focus on you and on performing a task.

Creeping on the down-stay. Return and use a two-handed, horizontal jerk backward.

Must be physically positioned on the sit or down. Give the sit and down commands randomly when your dog is on lead. If she doesn't obey immediately, use the two-handed upward jerk to correct for the sit and a forceful downward jerk for the down. Praise heavily, release and repeat. Sometimes try it in the house rather than during practice sessions.

Following you or moving out of position. Pivot to face your dog, grab the tab, lead or collar (use two hands for medium or large dogs) and swing her back into position. Then give the sit or down correction before leaving again.

Standing, sitting or downing before handler returns. Run in to correct with a jerk up for this sit or down for the down.

Downing submissively when you return on the long sit. Return in an arc for several weeks so you aren't walking toward your dog head-on. Keep circling her and gradually make your circles smaller. Tickle under her chin frequently when you return. If she goes down, walk in and lift her into a sit by the collar, but don't touch her body.

Moving after the return but before being released. Practice praising your dog and then walking around her several times before releasing her. Correct any movement with a jerk. Sometimes walk around her and back out front. Wait several seconds before returning and releasing.

IN THE RING

Responsibility of the Dog

- Sit on command.
- Down on command.
- Stay in position without making noise until released.

Responsibility of the Handler

- Make sure your dog is in a decent spot—not sitting on a rock or a red anthill (move the rock; report the anthill).
- Place your armband and lead so that your number is visible and the weight of your lead keeps the armband in place.
- Do not touch your dog to make her sit or down unless she gives you no choice. If you must place her, do it calmly and as gently as possible.
- Give commands and signals exactly as you give them when practicing.
- Step off on your right foot when leaving your dog.
- When facing your dog from across the ring, use the same posture and stance you use during practice.
- Don't fidget. It could be construed as a double command.
- Return around your dog smoothly and beware of stepping on her tail.

Common Handler Errors and Simple Corrections

Touching dog or collar. Try a second command before resorting to placing your dog in position. You do not lose points for repeating a command on the group exercises as long as your dog responds before she holds up the exercise.

Petting dog that broke the stay. If your dog ends up with you on the handler's side of the ring, don't absentmindedly pet her or she will feel praised for goofing off. Instead, with a minimum of fuss and no verbal command, place her right in front of you in the position she broke.

Giving commands differently than when practicing. Harsher than normal tones could make your dog feel insecure, and a dog needs confidence to maintain a stay.

Using body English from across the ring. Do not go into contortions to

make your dog stay. Chances are your dog won't notice but the judge will.

Not returning all the way to heel position.

Varying your stand. You may stand with your arms at your sides or folded. Just use the same position in the ring that your dog is used to seeing at practice.

Passing

To pass the sit, your dog must sit in place, without being noisy, from the time you leave until you are back in heel position. To pass the down, she must stay down and in place (no creepy crawling), quietly, until you return and release.

Following the down, the judge will tell each handler if the dog did or did not qualify.

Show Business: Novice

Before You Enter

- Watch and memorize the Novice routine at shows or matches to familiarize yourself with judging procedure and learn the difference between passing, failing and winning performances.
- Read and understand the rules. Write to the American Kennel Club, 51 Madison Ave., New York, N.Y. 10010, and request a free copy of the *Obedience Regulations.*
- Try your dog in practice matches and/or unfamiliar, distracting surroundings. She should consistently perform as well as you hope she performs at shows.
- Experiment with holding your lead in at your waist, side and in either hand to see if it affects your dog's performance. This will ensure that you don't lose unnecessary points for a tight lead. After deciding on a hand position, maintain it in the ring until the exercise is finished.
- To prepare your dog to perform as she does in training, regardless of ring conditions, practice:
  - —on different surfaces. Even shows advertised as indoor may be held in open-sided structures or on dirt floors.
  - —around birds. Many shows have a feathered audience chirping and flapping in the beams.
  - —over flashes of light on the floor created by bright sun shining through

windows into the ring. Many dogs try to avoid or jump them. If you don't have the real thing, use a flashlight to simulate the effect.

—lining up for exercises on different spots on the mat. See if your dog heels or finishes better when you are standing in the middle or toward the edge of the mat, but prepare her to perform regardless of what part of the mat she is on. Judges don't always time their commands, so you end up in the perfect spot and another dog may soil the ring, forcing you to line up or heel in a less-than-ideal place.

—around chalk marks, tape and on different surfaces encountered in the ring.

—varying the interval between commands to make allowances for the speed at which various judges will call commands. Sometimes call your dog right after turning around to face her on the recall and other times count silently to five before calling. Teach your dog to listen to your commands rather than just patterning her into a routine.

At the Show

- Check in and pick up your armband from the table steward located at the entrance of your ring.
- Arrive early enough to watch the pattern to see where and how the judge gives commands.
- Be ready and nearby when the previous dog is on the recall.

When It's Your Turn

- After marking the previous dog, the judge will get your score sheet, check your number, invite you into the ring, tell you where to line up, announce the exercise and ask if you are ready.
- Line up squarely on the mats. Walk a straight line while heeling and give your dog enough room to finish after the recall.
- Don't come to a screeching halt or change pace abruptly. To ease into a smooth transition, take a step or two before responding to the judge's orders. If turning immediately on the judge's command would make you heel off the mat when no one else did, turn a step or two after the judge calls the turn.
- Jerking or bumping with your knee or foot is prohibited. Physically placing or positioning your dog with your hand and/or lead, except on the stand, may be considered rough handling. Train your dog to line up easily and promptly with minimal fussing (see "Turning it Blue— Heeling on Lead," page 131).
- You will not risk losing points on lineups between exercises by:

  —patting your leg to encourage your dog into position.

—running over to set up points if it helps motivate your dog.

—heeling your dog to the lineup point if she needs to be kept under control.

—having a steady, taut lead without jerking.

—talking to your dog before telling the judge you are ready to begin.

- Put the lead back on before leaving the ring and ask when the long sit and down will be.

- You may leave after the long sit and down, but if the judge tells you that you've qualified, you will probably want to stay to get your score and qualifying ribbon and possibly a placement or special award. (Check the premium list for a complete list of special awards.)

- Tie scores for placements are broken by runoffs with the tied dogs each performing the off-lead heeling pattern.

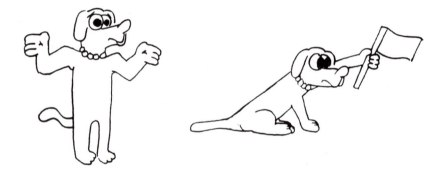

Say What?

Dogs live for the moment. When your dog breaks a stay and you tell her to come so you can take her to the breaking point and give a stay correction, she thinks she got a stay correction for coming. If she runs past you on the recall and you stop her with a down command so you can give a front correction when you get to her, she thinks she was corrected for downing. Canceling one command with another is like playing an elusive shell game with your dog's mind—a game she can never win. When your dog fails to execute a command, remain silent and use your hands to guide or correct her. And remember, lines allow you to keep control during the learning stage so that you can always enforce your commands.

NOVICE:
Turning It Blue

Heeling on Lead

HEELING CAN BE a pleasant way to walk your dog or an art form where the two of you appear to dance smoothly around the ring in perfect time.

PERFECTING THE FINE POINTS

Head Cues

You don't need the coordination of a gymnast or the concentration of a chess champion to improve teamwork and attention. Just look where you are going and your head cues will subtly indicate your intentions to your dog.

When changing direction, look in the new direction a step or two before turning. Of course, on the about turn you'll just look right, since only giraffes look good with their feet pointed north while their eyes look south. Soon your dog will realize that she can avoid corrections by watching for cues. She may even think she's getting away with something, but that's okay. Figuring out the system is a step in the right direction.

To indicate changes of pace, look at your feet when reducing speed and straight ahead to increase speed. Look down on halts, slow pace and coming out of fast pace. Look up on the forward, fast pace and when resuming normal pace after the slow. Don't cheat by twisting to stare at your dog. Cues must look and feel natural to be considered good, honest handling.

How can you give head cues and still know where your dog is? You still have to know when to correct, so monitor your dog by feeling where the lead is hitting your leg. If your lead is in your right hand against your outer thigh with just enough slack to be loose when your dog is in heel position, you will feel tension across the front of your legs whenever your dog lags or goes wide.

You can also see your dog through peripheral vision. Forging is easy to see and slipping out of view indicates lagging and/or wideness.

Stroll, or "Away We Go!"

Teach your dog to make an immediate, smooth transition into the slow pace by slowing down abruptly, then using the "Jackie Gleason left turn" to correct forging (see forging corrections in "Earning the Green," page 78). Once your dog is attentive to changes of pace, your halts will improve.

The "Jackie Gleason left turn" can also be used when you come to a stop and your dog doesn't, or if she turns into you on halts.

Lining Up to Begin an Exercise

Although you aren't scored on lineups, sloppiness in the ring could carry over into the next exercise. Teach precise lineups by suspensefully teasing, "Ready? You ready? Let's go!" then charge to a predetermined starting point. If your dog doesn't keep up with you, insist on promptness with a jump. Command "Sit" softly as you stop and correct, as you would during heeling.

Ready or Not?

The judge always asks if you are ready immediately before heeling patterns. Why not respond to the judge and cue your dog to watch at the same time? When your dog is distracted, eagerly say "Ready." If you've preceded running to lineups with "Ready, you ready?" your dog will probably look keenly. Eye contact is desirable but not necessary. Praise and insist she continue watching until you either release her or begin heeling. If she doesn't look toward you say "Uh" as you jerk the lead. If she still won't look, jump to the right and praise.

Say "Ready" only when the judge's next instruction will be "Forward." Respond to the judge with "Yes," or a head nod on nonheeling exercises.

Wrap Around About-Turns

Good heeling dogs curl around their handler on about-turns. Your dog will stay closer if she can't predict how far you'll turn, so encourage closeness by making another quarter turn to the right instead of stepping forward after the about-turn. Jump out of the turn, throw a toy in the new direction and take a short play break.

Planning turns next to a thin, solid pole can do wonders. After passing the pole on your right side, turn 180 degrees to the right so you will pass the pole on your left. Your dog will stay in close to avoid hitting the pole as you complete the turn. Also try passing the pole on your left, then doing an about-turn followed by a right turn in place to create a tighter wrap (270 degrees).

Inattention

Beginning heeling without establishing attention through sneakaways (see "Sneakaway Sessions," page 33) will get you as far as leaving for an unknown destination without studying a map first. Once your dog is distraction-proof on sneakaways, correct every time she glances away by using right and left turn corrections or halting with an automatic sit correction. If that doesn't work on your dog, you may have to use a prong collar, correct for every glance away, then break off and play. Hard corrections and exciting play should show your dog that you are the only game in town.

Pinpointing Position

Pinpointing will give your dog a better comprehension of heel position and help her lineups, sits and finishes.

Backing up: With your dog in heel position, hold the lead in your left hand, on or near the braiding. Command "Reverse" and step back with your left leg. Then jerk the lead back horizontally and bump your dog's chest with your right calf.

Tucking into position: To tuck your dog into position, hold the lead taut at your right side and sidestep right as you command "Tuck." As your left foot moves into position, sweep your dog's rear into a straight close sit with your left hand, then give her a friendly swat and a tickle on her left thigh so she is glad to be close.

Wideness

The tuck is also used to correct wideness while heeling. Just sidestep right and tuck your dog into a sit next to your leg as you halt.

Left U-turns also correct wideness. Pivot in place 180 degrees to the left as you tighten the lead and don't walk around your dog. Take up all the slack in your lead as you pivot or your dog will end up on your right. She should end up in an awkward position in front of your knees and have to scurry to get back where she belongs. Ultimately, she will learn that it is easier and more comfortable to stay close than to get back to heel position if you turn hard left.

To teach your dog to back up, step back with your left leg as you command "Reverse." Then jerk the lead back with your left hand as you tap your dog on the chest with your right calf.

Starting to teach the tuck.

134

MOTIVATION

Rev up your routine by playing immediately after a nice turn, change of pace or difficult maneuver. Say your release word, turn to face your dog and throw your arms up as you launch into a romp.

To encourage looking up, scratch medium and large dogs under the chin lightly and briefly with your left hand while heeling. Praise a good effort.

PROOFING

Heel into and along side walls, ropes and gates with your dog on the inside as well as the outside. If your dog lags when you are approaching a barrier, but you are too close to jump straight ahead, turn right and jump as she lags, then break off and praise.

Sometimes judges call commands late, so practice making smooth transitions from fast or slow back to normal when you are closing in on a barrier.

HANDLING

If you have been insisting on good lineups in practice, there is no need to grab your dog's collar or pat your leg between exercises at the show. You may run to your lineup points if that improves your dog's enthusiasm.

Use head cues to indicate turns, halts and changes of pace, but don't exaggerate your natural tendency to look where you are walking.

Bring your feet together on the about-turn and take a half step coming in and out of turns.

Practicing head cues and half steps should help you work out consistent footwork that your dog can easily follow. Check by asking the opinion of a respected fellow trainer or watch yourself on videotape.

Correct bumping or forging on the left post of the figure eight by pivoting left so that the post is on your right after your turn. Then halt and start over.

Correct lagging or wideness on the right post by pivoting right so that the post is on your dog's left side after you turn. Jump into the lead immediately following the turn. Then motivate.

Use the curly Q to teach your dog to wrap around you on the right post of the figure eight.

Keep your hands in front of your knees and circle 360 degrees in place to make the curly Q.

136

Figure Eight on Lead

IN PERFORMING the figure eight, your dog will not only have to maintain heel position on turns but will also have to make abrupt changes of pace.

PERFECTING THE FINE POINTS

Correct when your dog makes a mistake, then break out of the figure eight and start over. For instance, if your dog bumps you when circling the inside post, pivot hard left and either swing your left leg toward her shoulder or march into her if she is in your path. Halt after she scurries out of your way, then praise and run back to your lineup point to start over.

Emphasize changes of pace by slowing down around the left-turn post and speeding up abruptly to normal on the straightaway and around the right post. Motivate by praise as you increase your pace.

MOTIVATION

If your dog lags, turn right, then puddle jump until she is running up to position. If you turn far enough, she will be between you and the post when you jump. Break off heeling by turning to face your dog, then back up and motivate with happy talk, push-play or a toy.

Use head cues on the figure eight by looking in the direction you plan to go. Don't twist your torso. The cues must be subtle and feel natural.

Look at the opposite post to cue your dog to slow down or speed up.

When your dog heels around both posts beautifully, encourage her to wrap around your leg on the right-hand post by finishing with a curly Q. As you complete the outside turn, bring your hands in front of your knees and circle in place 360 degrees to the right as you cheer her on. Then back away from her and encourage her to play.

PROOFING

Proof by heeling around posts that are only three feet from a wall or baby gate. Occasionally the judge may be forced to position the posts close to a barrier because of lack of matting.

Stewards don't always stand exactly eight feet apart, so practice distances from six feet to ten feet.

Practice halts on every straightaway and every curve.

HANDLING

Look in the direction you plan to start (left or right) before giving the heel command. Always start in the same direction. Dogs usually heel more precisely starting to the left.

When halting on a curve, slow down in a straight line. Your dog will have difficulty sitting straight if you are arcing.

Look at your feet one step before slowing down to cue your dog that you are stopping.

Give a head cue to indicate your starting direction when continuing after a halt. While circling one post, smoothly look toward the other. There is no rule that says you can't look where you are going. You do it naturally when walking around your home or office but probably become rigid in the obedience ring. Loosen up, relax, shake your head—and move it subtly to give head cues.

If the figure eight is on the width of one mat, try to keep your dog on the mat so she doesn't lose her footing and go wide. Do a "teardrop" figure eight (which looks like a left and right U-turn and two straightaways) by cutting closer to the side of the post and leaving more distance between you and the back of the post.

The Great Dane, Am., Can. Ch. Danehaven's Rolling Thunder, Canadian OTCH, UDT, TDX also has a CD at United Kennel Club trials, a WDX, HC and is a member of TDI (Therapy Dogs International). He is owned and trained by Marta Brock.

Heel Free

IF YOUR DOG HEELS WELL with the lead behind your back and catches up quickly off lead when you jump ahead, you are ready to bring her up to her potential.

PERFECTING THE FINE POINTS

When you become a perfectionist your intensity can make your dog feel insecure about heeling, so it is best to demand more from her on informal lineups first. Insisting on quick, precise lineups off lead will improve lagging and sitting problems. Say "Ready? You ready? Let's go!" and take off to your destination. Correct when your dog isn't running at the same speed you are or if she starts to fall behind. Occasionally release and play after an eager run. Otherwise, stop and be prepared to correct for poor sits as described in "Earning the Green—Heeling on Lead," page 73.

"But She Knows When the Lead Is Off"

All the on-lead work in the world won't change a dog who sparkles on lead but is lackluster off lead. The problem must be corrected where it exists—off lead. Sure the corrections are less direct and slower, but if your dog is fantastic on lead, she obviously knows heel position and will grasp your message in spite of a slight delay.

Lagging

Once your dog lags, do not speed up to give a hurried correction. If she corrects herself, she should be praised. Slow down and correct in a way that makes your dog think instead of just reacting.

Stop as soon as your dog leaves position, walk up to the tab and jerk it with your left hand as you step forward again and praise. Repeat the pattern that made your dog lag in the first place, and when she does it once successfully, release and play. If your dog continues repeating the mistake or gets worse, release and play after the correction and work on a different exercise. Then come back to the sticky place again and be ready to correct and motivate. Soon your dog should regain her confidence on that exercise and be eager for your motivation.

Wideness

Stop, walk to the tab and sidestep to the right and slightly forward as you pull your dog into a sit by your leg. Praise by tickling her left thigh.

The collar can also be used to correct. Sometimes grabbing a buckle collar is more effective and directional than using the tab.

PROOFING

Practice lineups and short segments of heeling (less than thirty seconds) when your dog least expects it, such as on walks and when she is playing in the yard. Teaching her to focus on you and change her priorities and frame of mind at a second's notice will help her perform well without a warm-up. So, when you are unexpectedly called in for a runoff or arrive at a show and have to perform right away because of absentees, your dog will be ready even if you aren't. Play with her after random lineups and heeling so she will enjoy being part of your spontaneity.

HANDLING

Have someone watch to make sure your head cues are natural.

Discover the pace and stride that best complement your dog. Most dogs work best when handlers use a slightly shorter and brisker stride than their normal walk. Make smooth, gradual transitions into and out of the fast and slow paces. Try not to be so nervous in the ring that you respond abruptly to the judge's command. Handling like that makes maintaining heel position about as easy as catching a jumping flea.

Walk in a straight line by following the mat or glancing at a point straight ahead of you if there is no mat. Keep your feet under you, roll from heel to ball and push off from your toes. You'll have better balance and be smoother than if you were landing flat-footed.

If your dog has a tendency to bump, try heeling with your left arm swinging.

Recall

T HERE ARE FIVE COMPONENTS to this exercise: the stay, the response to your command, moving toward you, the front and the finish—and each part provides its own training challenges.

PERFECTING THE FINE POINTS

Response

To achieve a quicker response to your call, be demanding when calling your dog in the house. Although you aren't asking her to sit, if you impress her with the importance of responding promptly to a come command, even when she isn't training, it will have a positive carryover effect. Don't let her dillydally on the way to you either.

Outdoors, try practicing with people walking around and through your recall and in fields with lots of tempting scents. Correct for sniffing with a rap under the jaw, then jerk toward you as you continue walking backward.

To add enthusiasm and speed, leave your dog on a sit, walk about twenty feet away and turn as if you were about to call her. But instead of calling, turn and walk about ten feet more before facing her again. If you look down to square up your feet before calling your dog, do that while practicing this technique too. Sometimes walk away and turn and line yourself up a few times before calling.

"Thinner thighs in thirty recalls" position. Make a pocket with your knees, keep your back straight and hold the collar from under your dog's chin to keep her head up. If you need to guide her closer or straighter, use your other hand on her back.

Pointing out the front. Bend your knees and point with two fingers to make a frame. Avoid pointing with one hand or your dog will learn to focus on your hand instead of a spot on your middle.

Center your toes against the front board of the front box. The box should be just wide enough to fit snugly next to your dog's rear.

The longer wait and the suspense of wondering how far you will go could make your dog hustle when she finally gets your command.

Try running your dog to your lineup point. You can do that in the ring as well.

If your dog still ambles in, use various distractions while she is in transit from the stay to the front. Try bones, squeaky toys, open car doors and gates. If she detours, correct as you would for not coming in at all.

If all else fails to speed your dog's recall, and you are sure she is just lazy, not insecure or distracted, correct ambling in by walking up to her collar and jerking as you back up and praise. Release the collar and continue backing and praising.

Thinner Thighs in Thirty Recalls Position

Getting a consistent, straight front with no bumping can be challenging and time-consuming. When training a medium-sized or larger dog, make a pocket of your body by bending your knees and hold your dog's collar under her chin. Keep your back straight and take no steps in toward your dog, but pull her toward you as you back up until she is straight. If she tries to swing her rear to the side, guide it with your hand as you pull her in. This technique teaches your dog where to focus when coming in and encourages her to be close.

The Front Box

When your dog comes in without resistance, a front box will help her into position without the aid of your hands. Make it out of one-by-two-inch or two-by-four-inch boards. It should be just wide enough for your dog to sit in and about a foot longer than her rear when she is sitting with her front feet at the front board. The more likely she is to want to sit on the sides, the higher the sides should be.

To introduce your dog to the front box, walk her through it on a tight lead until she seems comfortable with it. Then heel her so that her front legs are in the box and put her on a sit-stay. Keep doing sit-stays closer to the front of the box until her feet are against the front board.

When she is used to being all the way in the box, put her on a sit-stay with just her front feet in the box, position yourself so that your toes are centered and against the board, and call your dog front using the lead to help her into position. Gradually place her farther away from the box and call her in. Eventually practice angling the opening of the box away from your dog so that she has to maneuver. Be ready to step in and make her come through the box rather than alongside it.

Increase the distance little by little until your dog does a fifty-foot recall into the front box with no help from you.

You will practice eventually without the front box. There is no real cor-

Fixing a front. If your dog is sitting in front of one of your legs instead of centered, back up with the opposite leg. She will have to walk around the leg she was in front of and should end up in a straight front.

Hold a toy under your chin. Then call your dog front and drop the toy as you release her.

rection for crooked fronts. It is simply a matter of making your dog work herself into a straight front, then practice and more practice. Incessantly nit-picking fronts leads to tentative, slow recalls. Allow more leeway in the precision department and gradually, as your dog's confidence grows, you can begin demanding more perfection.

Banishing Bumps

Avoid bumping by teaching your dog to come in with her head up. Use the "thinner thighs" position, placing your hand on her collar under her chin to teach her to walk into a sit with her head up. Then use her favorite toy to make her want to do it alone. Get her interested in the toy, then back up as you hold it at chin level for a medium or large dog or waist level for a small dog. When your dog is walking close in front of you and looking at the toy, drop it as you release her. After a dozen or so of those (more for an uninterested dog, less for an enthusiastic one), command "Sit" and stop. Keep the lead taut to ensure good position, then drop the toy with an exuberant release. Start putting the toy under your chin, so that your hands are at your sides as your dog comes in. Then drop it as you release. Besides bringing her head up, using the toy will help your dog map out a focal point and improve her attention.

The Finish

If your dog starts cutting short, making sitting straight difficult, take her collar and guide her behind your left leg before allowing her to turn and complete the finish.

If she takes the scenic route when finishing, be ready to throw a sky hook when she is gaping around and use the tab to jerk her into heel position.

Set up the front box in finish position to pattern your dog into finishing accurately.

To speed up a tentative finish or add precision to a dog who is just a little off, hold food in your left hand and offer it after she sits. This technique only works on small and medium-sized dogs who are interested in food enough to care but not enough to forget to sit.

MOTIVATION

Insist that your dog remain attentive after coming into the front or an interesting distraction could make her miss the finish. At first, have her remain in front position only a split second before releasing her with enthusiasm. Gradually increase the duration. The lively release your dog is waiting for should hold her attention. If it doesn't, say "Uh" and give a quick snap upward on the lead. If that doesn't work, review "Sneakaway Sessions," page 33.

If your dog is tentative, practice formal, ring-style recalls with lively play afterward. Build excitement by adding suspense, as explained in "Response." Familiarity will increase confidence and speed. Also practice calling her to front around the house and yard when she least expects it.

Increase speed by practicing one finish before feeding or exercising. The pleasant activity that follows plus the confidence that comes with more practice is apt to enliven your dog's performance.

PROOFING

Add distractions to increase speed and attention.

Judges differ on how they call commands, so count different lengths of time before calling, praising, finishing and releasing.

Get a friend to help you proof by loudly calling other commands, like down and come (but not directly at your dog or using her name) as you practice the recall.

Get a friend to serve as judge, and run through the whole recall. After the "judge" says, "Finish your dog," either wait until the count of three to command the finish or fake out your dog by twisting your upper body, bending your knees or coughing. Be ready to correct with an upward jerk.

HANDLING

Place your feet straight forward to give your dog a better chute to line up with. When you turn around in the ring, look at your feet to make sure you've spaced them properly (the same as in practice) and they are straight. Then look up at your dog or the judge.

In the ring, leave plenty of room beside you and behind you for your dog to finish, but practice with barriers close behind and beside you anyway.

When practicing on mats, experiment with lining up on various spots to see if this makes a difference in how your dog sits and finishes. Utilize that knowledge in the ring.

Steady She Stays

TREAT EVERY STAY as if it were being scored and correct accordingly. If you casually command "Stay" around the house or kennel and then ignore creeping, scratching, shaking, sniffing and noisemaking, your dog will learn bad habits that could carry over into the ring.

AVOIDING AND CORRECTING MOVEMENT PROBLEMS

When your dog no longer falls for distractions, stays solidly, knows the stand-stay and holds for a thorough exam, even when people talk to her, begin insisting that she keep her paws still on the sit-stay. Start on lead, stand three feet away from her and put a little horizontal pressure on the lead. If your dog moves a paw, say "Uh" as you slide your free hand down the lead and jerk up. The lead should have constant tension on it during the procedure. When your dog resists a little pressure, return and praise.

Some dogs get into trouble because they watch the rest of the group. That is fine when all the dogs are doing well, but it leaves too much to luck. It is not necessary to practice both the sit-stay and the down-stay every time you train with a group. One is sufficient and not overly boring. When you do two stays, follow the "25 percent rule" to teach your dog not to anticipate but to remember instructions:

- 25 percent of the time—two sit-stays
- 25 percent of the time—two down-stays
- 25 percent of the time—one down-stay followed by one sit-stay
- 25 percent of the time—one standard sit-stay followed by one down-stay

HANDLING

Although your dog is already sitting when the judge says, "Sit your dogs," say, "Orbit, sit," anyway. That cues your dog that this is the long sit and you are ready to correct even minor movement.

If you have never commanded your dog to sit while she was already sitting, or if she has never heard a group of handlers give a sit command in unison, she is likely to go down. If she downs when practicing with a group, simply pull her into a sit silently, praise her with a pat on the chest and repeat until she is no longer confused.

When practicing in a line with other dogs, occasionally move your dog. A judge may decide to reposition you in the ring, so she should be easy to move verbally and should settle into a new position quickly.

OPEN:
Earning the Green

Drop on Recall

Prerequisites

When your dog is reliable amid distractions on the Novice recall and you can down her on the first command without touching her, she is ready to learn to drop on recall.

You may be tempted to scream the command, so test your dog's hearing before teaching the moving drop. See how far away, even with the TV playing, your dog can hear you fixing her dinner. Then remind yourself to give the down command clearly, but no louder than the command to come.

What's New?

As your dog moves toward you on a recall, the judge will signal you to down her. On your command, she should drop immediately and completely—not just crouch. Your dog must remain in position until the judge tells you to call her and you give the command to come. Then she should get right up, move toward you briskly and sit in front.

The only two new moves are downing in motion and coming out of the down to do a recall, but expect some confusion when you teach this exercise. While your dog is learning it, her Novice recall will probably slow down. Don't worry about it, and don't try to speed it up. When she understands the exercise, her speed will probably return.

Relationship to Conformation

This exercise does not relate to anything in the breed ring. It relates to life. Coming when called and stopping immediately on command are two of the most important exercises your dog can learn to ensure her safety.

Equipment

You will need the collar and lead plus your longe and light lines.

TEACHING THE EXERCISE

Begin by downing your dog randomly, on lead. Say her name and "Down," when she is casually walking around with you and during training. Insist that she drop exactly where she was when you gave the command. If she takes a few steps before downing, use the lead to swing her back to where she was and jerk her down. Then back away while softly praising her.

When your dog does random drops well on lead, increase your distance by tying her to a post. Walk ten feet from her and give the down command in a firm and somber, but not loud, tone. Correct when necessary with a downward jerk, two-handed for stronger dogs.

When your dog does reliable random drops in a training situation, begin practicing them around the house and yard. Enforce immediately, then praise and release.

Connecting the Pieces

When you have added distractions and your dog will drop promptly anywhere, anytime, she is ready to learn the formal drop on recall. Begin on lead by calling her, then dropping her immediately. Return and praise her or, if necessary, correct the same way as for random drops. As she progresses, gradually increase the distance to longe line length.

Once your dog is dropping reliably and quickly, call her in about one-third of the time after praising her verbally for dropping. One-third of the time call her in without praising her first and, for the other third, return to your dog while she is down, praise her and release. Add new distractions, attach the light line and gradually increase the distance to around the thirty-five feet you will have in the ring. If she starts dropping slowly to get a head start on the recall, return to her instead of calling her. When she is reliable with distractions, begin practicing off lead.

Anticipation Prevention

To keep your dog from trying to drop before you give the command, don't drop her every time you do a recall. Alternate the straight Novice recall with the drop on recall and add an occasional fake out.

Fake Outs

To fake out your dog, begin by softly saying the first sound in your dog's name. For a name like Manchita, say "Man," when she is halfway to you. If she slows down, that is good, because it means she's thinking. If she stops completely, calmly reel her in and praise.

Common Errors of the Dog and Simple Corrections

Not downing or not going all the way down. Run in and give as strong a downward jerk as necessary to make your point.

Slow drop. Use new distractions to make your dog forget what she is doing. Then correct for no drop by swinging her back to where she received the command and giving a solid downward jerk.

Sniffing or fooling with the grass. Upward cuff under the chin and practice the exercise using plenty of aromatic distractions.

Taking steps before downing or creeping after she is down. As soon as you see that your dog is not stopping in her tracks, move in fast to swing her back to where you gave the command. Jerk down, move away and praise.

Getting up from the down before the command. Swing your dog back into position and jerk her down. Variety usually cures this problem, so return to your dog frequently instead of calling her in from the drop and sometimes praise her before calling her in after she drops.

Slow response. If this exercise is new to your dog, ignore slowness. It often improves after your dog understands the exercise. If it doesn't improve, practice short recalls following the down in nontraining situations. For example, after a walk, or after your dog comes in from the yard, do a random down, go about six feet away from her and call her. Correct by walking up to her collar and jerking, then back up and use lots of praise if your dog is trotting. Try it again in a few hours, rather than drilling it and making your dog worry. Worry is a major cause of slowness.

IN THE RING

Responsibility of the Dog

- Sit-stay and regular Novice recall.

- Down on command while moving and stay until called.
- Recall from down position.
- Front and finish.

Responsibility of the Handler

Same as in the Novice recall.

Common Errors of the Handler and Simple Corrections

Identical to those in the Novice recall.

Nodding her down. You may down your dog with a verbal command or a hand signal, but not both. Be careful of body English. Your head and maybe the whole top half of your body is going to want to nod as you call, "Down."

Passing

If your dog stays until you call her, comes on command, drops all the way down on command or signal, stays down until your next command and comes to within easy touching distance after you call, she will probably pass. If her responses are slow or she takes a few steps before downing, the judge will take points off. If "incredibly slow" best describes her responses, she may fail.

Retrieving Woes

I, JACQUELINE FRASER, am going to try to convince you to use force when training your dog to retrieve—something no one could talk me into with my first Open dog. Beau was an American Staffordshire Terrier. He loved chasing a tennis ball, brought it back most of the time and sometimes even released it. Other times I had to pry it loose. I thought I could transfer Beau's delight in tennis balls to dumbbells, and soon, when he was in the mood, he would pick one up by the end and trot back with it dangling from the side of his mouth. Although the rules do not mention how to hold the dumbbell, I knew it would fall out of his mouth on the high jump if he carried it that way, so I tried to teach him to carry it by the middle. He tilted his head back, eased the dowel between his molars, clamped down and broke it so that the ends fell off. Over the next few weeks he bit two more dumbbells into thirds. It was expensive and frustrating, but the worst part was that Beau was being corrected so often that he decided retrieving wasn't fun anymore. Sometimes he ignored my command to take the dumbbell, and since I had no way to enforce it, I resorted to bribery. I rubbed liver bait on the dowel and had a piece of the real thing ready to give Beau when he returned with the dumbbell. But he didn't return. He licked it and pushed it around and when he was satisfied that the good taste was gone, he discarded it like a piece of used chewing gum.

I'd like to think that everyone, not just me, can remember an incident that marked their personal low point in dog training. Mine occurred when I decided that Beau generally tried to please; the problem was that he didn't understand.

With that I bought a new dumbbell, knelt down to his eye level and put it in my own mouth to show him how to hold it. Beau was not impressed, but if the neighbors were watching, I'm sure they were.

Weeks passed and I nagged and badgered Beau until he retrieved most of the time. Finally he could retrieve on the flat and over the high jump. He still held the dumbbell by the end sometimes, but seldom dropped it, even when jumping.

Beau qualified on his first and third try. He bombed on his second because awards were being presented in the next ring, the applause attracted his attention and he forgot to retrieve. Going for his final leg, he dropped the dumbbell just before the jump, picked it up and leaped over awkwardly from a standstill.

"Lucky," the judge said.

I did feel lucky and a little smug. Everyone had said I'd never earn a CDX without force training my dog and I did it anyway.

Later I discovered that my determination to train Beau without physical force had mental repercussions. By incessantly nagging him about retrieves, I had ruined his favorite sport. Beau never brought anyone a tennis ball to throw for him again, and if we threw one anyway, he returned it listlessly with resignation in his eyes.

Eta, the next dog I trained for Open, never retrieved anything for fun. I used a force method called the "ear pinch" on her and she learned to return a dumbbell correctly for praise. Soon, retrieving anything, from sticks to rubber duckies, became her favorite amusement. So "fun" retrieving took the fun out of Beau's retrieve and force training turned Eta on to a new game.

If you absolutely can't bring yourself to cause your dog any discomfort— even for a second, even after trying it on yourself and realizing it isn't agonizing—you may also get lucky and your dog may qualify in Open anyway. But if you want your dog to learn quickly, with praise and without nagging, try force. It does the job and leaves you with a correction to rely on when necessary.

We are presenting only the force method here, because the "fun" method can't be taught. Your dog will either feel like retrieving in the ring or she won't. She may feel like it at home when there is nothing better to do but ignore her dumbbell amid distractions. Without a correction there is no solution to that problem, so if you decide to rely on "fun" retrieves, we hope you get lucky too.

Retrieve on the Flat

Prerequisites

Your dog is ready to learn retrieving when she is solid on the sit-stay and the recall.

What's New?

Up until now, every time your dog performed an exercise at a distance from you, it was you who left her and called her back to you. When retrieving, your dog leaves you and returns automatically.

This is also the first exercise where your dog picks up, carries and releases an object on command.

Relationship to Conformation

As long as the word *show* is in dog show, creative exhibitors will find a way to display a reliable retrieving dog, especially if she is not a natural retrieving breed. Imagine a Boxer carrying its owner's catalog to ringside or a Whippet leaving the ring with her Group rosette dangling proudly from her mouth. People love to watch a dog do something different, even silly, as long as it looks like the dog's idea and does not interfere with another dog (see "The [Controlled] Brat," page 57).

To place the dumbbell in your dog's mouth, hold it by the end with one hand and use your other hand to open her mouth. Insert your fingers behind her upper canine teeth as you do when opening her mouth to give her a pill.

Cup your dog's muzzle for a second before allowing her to release the dumbbell. Hold the back of her head if she tries to mouth the dumbbell (jiggle it around in her mouth).

Equipment

Your dog will retrieve a wooden dumbbell. These are available in a variety of styles, and it is important that the length and height of the dumbbell fit your dog's size and mouth contours.

The length of the dowel (the portion between the ends) should be no more than one-half inch longer than the width of your dog's mouth. With a short-muzzled breed like the Pug, or a breed with pendulous flews like the Blood-hound, be particularly careful that her lips are not pinched tight against the ends.

The dumbbell's height off the floor should be sufficient to allow your dog to pick it up quickly without bumping her nose or her chin on the ground.

Your dog must have total visibility when carrying her dumbbell, so check that the bell portion doesn't cover her eyes.

Many people use dumbbells with the ends painted white because they are usually easier for the dog to see. If doing the painting yourself, *do not* paint the dowel.

The bell portion comes in various shapes. Squared-off ends seem to bounce and roll less than round ones and consequently land where aimed more often.

One is not enough. Dumbbells can break. Perversely, they have been known to last through months of practice and land in two or three pieces the first time thrown in the ring. Although your dog will be required to fetch one of the broken pieces, the judge will allow you to use a different dumbbell on the next retrieve. It is smart to have another dumbbell, exactly like the one your dog practiced on, ready for such an emergency. To be a viable spare, it should be slightly used, so it smells and feels natural to your dog.

TEACHING THE EXERCISE

Step One: Open Mouth, Insert Dumbbell

Start with your dog sitting. Open her mouth as if you were giving her a pill and command "Fetch," as you place the dumbbell in the space in front of her molars. Cup the dumbbell in her mouth, hold it in position for no more than two seconds and give soft praise. Command "Give" or "Out" or my personal favorite, "Thank you," and remove the dumbbell from her mouth. If your dog doesn't want to release it, pat one end with your palm as you hold the other end. Repeat this procedure twenty times a day for a full week or until your dog doesn't resist when you put the dumbbell in her mouth or take it out.

Step Two: Cooperation under Pressure

With your dog sitting, tighten her collar so it is high around her neck. The live ring should be running under her right ear and the excess chain is in your left hand. Hold the dumbbell by the end in your right hand, place the dowel against

Start using force when your dog no longer resists having the dumbbell placed in her mouth. Adjust the collar to fit snugly around the high part of her neck, hold it with your left hand and be ready to direct your dog's head if she won't take the dumbbell.

Excite your dog between retrieves by teasing her with the dumbbell, but don't let her get it in her mouth.

her teeth and push with moderate pressure while commanding "Fetch." If your dog doesn't open her mouth to take the dumbbell, use your left hand to tighten the chain by pulling it forward, toward the dumbbell. Now the dumbbell is exerting pressure on your dog's teeth while your left hand is exerting pressure on the lead to push her toward it. In this "no choice" position, you dog will eventually open her mouth and accept the dumbbell. As soon as she does, praise her, release the collar pressure and cup her muzzle for about five seconds. Even though your dog doesn't reach for the dumbbell on command, you will soon have to force for shorter and shorter periods before she opens her mouth.

If, before you give the fetch command, your dog moves out of the sit in anticipation of grabbing the dumbbell, restrain her with a tight lead and praise her as she settles in. Then set your lead and dumbbell up again.

Moving off the sit to grab the dumbbell on command is normal and calls for praise.

Use motivation between retrieves to lighten the air and pique your dog's interest in the dumbbell. After a few retrieves, do a push-play release and tease your dog with the dumbbell. Behave as if you just stole it—tap it on the ground and hide it behind your back. Don't let her take it. Just get her interested in it and then go back to work for a few minutes before playing again.

Step Three: The Ear Pinch

When your dog usually takes a dumbbell pressed lightly against her teeth, set her collar up as in step two, but place the excess chain against the fleshy part of the inside of your dog's ear. (For some dogs you may have to buy the next larger chain collar to reach.) Hold the chain in place with your left hand by keeping your thumb on top of her ear and your index finger under the chain.

Sit your dog, hold the dumbbell in front of her mouth and give the fetch command. If your dog takes the dumbbell, praise. Then set up distractions and try again. In order for your dog to become reliable on the retrieve, she will have to make mistakes and be corrected. If the distractions are interesting enough, eventually she will forget to take the dumbbell.

When your dog ignores or refuses her dumbbell, pinch her ear by squeezing your thumb and index finger against the chain and her ear. That should cause an uncomfortable enough sensation (try it on your own ear) to make her open her mouth. The instant she does, insert the dumbbell, stop the pressure, praise her and cup her mouth to keep the dumbbell in place. Wait a few seconds, give your command to take the dumbbell from her mouth and praise her again.

While some dogs get the point quickly and avoid an ear pinch by opening their mouths and reaching for the dumbbell upon hearing the fetch command, other dogs balk at this exercise. The secret is to be matter-of-fact and persistent. Enforce the sit by restraining the dog that is trying to anticipate and jerking the dog that is trying to leave. Train patiently and consistently. Never lose your temper or pull your dog's ear to get her to move toward the dumbbell. Eventually even the most stubborn dog will find it easier to do the exercise than to fight it. Remember, you already trained your dog to know what "fetch" means. The ear pinch is simply a correction.

Inch by Inch

When your dog opens her mouth on command, hold the dumbbell one inch away from her. By now she should move her head forward to take the dumbbell. If she doesn't reach for it, pinch her ear. Release the pressure and praise her when she takes it.

With a super-stubborn dog, you may have a "go-around" at this point. A go-around is when you hold the dumbbell an inch from her nose and pinch her ear and she either struggles or pretends the pinch isn't happening, but she does not move to take the dumbbell. Since the chain is tight around the highest part of her neck, you'll move your dog forward with the collar while you continue the ear pressure. Of course, you and the dumbbell will be moving forward too. As you keep the pressure on and she keeps balking, you may find yourselves going around in a circle. If you persist, she will take the dumbbell. Release the pressure and praise like crazy. By then, crazy will come easy.

What if you go around and around and she still won't take the dumbbell? Go back to step one and then remain at step two until you are certain she knows what is expected of her. Then work on the first part of step three, enforcing the sit and pinching when necessary with the dumbbell just in front of her muzzle, until she opens her mouth eagerly. When you move on, if she still won't reach an inch for the dumbbell, there are other methods besides the ear pinch. The collar twist is a reliable second choice. If your dog's ears are absolutely insensitive, and you must use the collar twist, learn it in the company of a professional dog trainer. A book can't watch you work and tell you how much is too much.

Once your dog reaches one inch forward and takes the dumbbell on command without a pinch, begin using more distractions and increase the distance slowly, inch by inch. When your dog is successful at arm's length, stop setting up for the ear pinch before you send her to fetch. From now on set up and pinch only after she refuses to retrieve. When your dog responds to the fetch command without your hand on her ear, she is ready to move on.

Step Four: Retrieving off the Ground

One of the most difficult transitions your dog will encounter during obedience training is between retrieving a dumbbell that you are holding and retrieving one off the ground. Gradually is the fastest way to accomplish it.

Start holding the dumbbell closer to the ground at almost arm's length. Lower it slowly until your dog will take it without correction (ear pinch) with you holding one end and the other end touching the ground. Then begin slowly tipping the dumbbell until it is all the way on the ground with your hand still-holding one end.

Tip the dumbbell when you first get to ground level so only one end is touching the ground.

Retrieving from a platform. This is an intermediate step before retrieving from the floor. If your dog refuses to open her mouth or turns her head away from the dumbbell despite the ear pinch, direct her head toward it with one hand on her skull and the other on her collar.

When your dog reliably fetches her dumbbell from the ground with your hand on it, remove your hand but point to the dumbbell with your finger only an inch from the end. Correct if necessary. Each time you practice, move your hand a little farther from the dumbbell until you can stand straight with your hand at your side.

Sometime during this transition, your dog may pretend she doesn't see her dumbbell or may turn away from it. Resist touching the dumbbell. Instead, maneuver her muzzle toward it with your hand on her skull and your middle finger on her stop. Your other hand should hold the collar tightly to direct her head. When her muzzle is lined up with her dumbbell, correct with an ear pinch even if she suddenly decides to reach for the dumbbell herself.

Once your dog picks her dumbbell off the ground by herself, you should never have to pick it up for her again. Train her to hold it while moving by backing up a step or two after she fetches and praising as she comes toward you with her dumbbell. Correct with an ear pinch if she drops it, but do not repeat the fetch command. She should remember that fetch means grab it and hold on to it until commanded otherwise. Gradually increase your steps backward and line her up for a nice front.

Step Five: Distance, Distractions and Variations

Occasionally practice the retrieve formally, even though you are still throwing the dumbbell only a little more than arm's length and your dog is still on lead.

Sit her at heel and give the command and signal to stay. Wait a second, then throw the dumbbell a few feet. Keep firm pressure on the lead if your dog is the type that anticipates and loosen it as you give the command to fetch. When your dog retrieves the dumbbell, praise and guide her into a sit in front. Hesitate a few seconds, then give the command to release the dumbbell to you. Take it and give the finish command.

Increase the distance foot by foot by going from lead to longe line to fifty-foot light line. Allow the line to run through your hand as you send your dog out but make sure you aren't stepping on it, as that would give an undeserved correction. Add distractions at every level. Throw the dumbbell under a chair or table. Have it land near a person who is petting a dog on the ground. Practice in new areas often. Don't send your dog every time you throw her dumbbell. Sometimes leave her on a sit-stay and go out to get the dumbbell yourself. Other times, throw the dumbbell and walk around your dog before you send her. When she is steady and retrieves reliably, remove the line but not the tab and begin off-lead work.

Put your dog back on line or lead or shorten your toss if you jumped ahead too fast and confused her.

Common Errors of the Dog and Simple Corrections

Failing to retrieve on the first try. Take your dog to new locations and do only one retrieve. Even though you probably had to correct, put your dog back in the car and drive somewhere else. Repeat for several training sessions until your dog consistently retrieves the first throw.

Failing to retrieve on the first command. Set the collar up for an ear pinch and walk her all the way to the dumbbell until she has her teeth around the dowel.

Slow response. Use distractions to make her forget entirely what she is doing. Then make a clear-cut correction as above.

Sniffing, playing, fooling around, dropping the dumbbell and failing to retrieve. Put your dog on the shortest lead or line possible where she will still make the error. Allow the lead or line to run through your hand as your dog goes out, so you can snub it up when the transgression occurs, and go hand over hand down the line to her. Set the collar up and use the ear pinch.

Mouthing or chewing the dumbbell. As your dog opens her mouth to chew, try to give the line a jerk so that the dumbbell falls out. Then snub up the line, set up the collar and give an ear pinch.

A practice dumbbell with a metal dowel will also change her mind about chewing and no correction will be needed.

Anticipating the fetch command. While teaching, if your dog gets grabby, tighten the lead or line until she settles back into a sit. Praise her and bring the dumbbell back down to your side. Repeat until your dog isn't grabby, then send.

Sometimes fake out your dog after you throw the dumbbell. Bend your knees, praise, cough or walk to the dumbbell yourself. Correct movement the same as if she broke any other sit-stay but with a gentler jerk. Praise after the correction.

Jumping the high jump. Put your dog on lead and do a retrieve right alongside the jump. If she tries to take the jump, maneuver her with a taut lead and praise. Practice the same thing on the light line and, if she tries to jump, say "Uh-uh" as you walk hand-over-hand down the line toward her. Then maneuver her the right way.

Use the retrieve command for the flat and a jump command for the high jump.

Making a slow return. Use distractions and correct with a jerk of the lead or line if your dog forgets what she is doing. If your dog is off lead, correct with a jerk on the tab.

Resentfully giving up the dumbbell. Hold the dumbbell with one hand and pat the end of it with the other.

Sitting out of reach, between feet, touching, poor or no front or finish. Use the corrections for the Novice recall and read "Fetching Fabulous Fronts" in the "blue" section of the retrieve on the flat (see page 160).

You won't lose points for a bad throw, but it does make it more difficult for your dog to maintain concentration.

IN THE RING

Responsibility of the Dog

- Sit-stay.
- Leave handler on retrieve command.
- Pick up the dumbbell.
- Automatically return carrying the dumbbell.
- Front holding the dumbbell.
- Release the dumbbell on command.
- Finish (return to heel position on command).

Responsibility of the Handler

- Issue clear commands, exactly as practiced.
- Keep your hands at your sides while the dog retrieves.
- Make a decent dumbbell toss (at least twenty feet and as straight as possible).
- Give the stay signal with your left hand and throw with your right (or vice versa, if necessary), but don't do both with the same hand.
- Bring a comfortably used dumbbell that is not mauled, chewed or cracked and have a handy spare.

Common Handler Errors and Simple Corrections

Making a poor throw. Tosses of less than twenty feet must be repeated, and throws outside the ring are also repeated. You won't lose points for a bad throw, but it does make it more difficult for your dog to maintain concentration. A diagonal toss, where your dumbbell lands in line with the high jump, may induce your dog to take the jump on her way back if it is the first thing she sees when she turns after the retrieve.

Practice throwing the dumbbell. Try snapping your wrist upward to add a little spin and see if that helps your aim and makes the dumbbell bounce less.

Passing

Your dog will probably pass if she waits until you send her, retrieves on the first command and brings the dumbbell back to within your reach. There are many ways to lose points. The most common are slow responses, pouncing or playing with the dumbbell, dropping it, touching the handler, jumping the high jump and having a poor front and finish. Your dog could make most (but probably not all) of these mistakes and still pass.

The Norwich Terrier, Ch. Dastropen Celestial Sprout, UD, owned by Sally Culley, taking the broad jump in good style. Terriers are often considered difficult to train in obedience. These dogs often need a different training approach, but they will definitely respond under the right conditions.

Retrieve Over the High Jump

Prerequisites

Your dog should perform the retrieve on the flat at least a lead length away, with distractions, before starting to retrieve over a jump.

What's New?

Since you are only allowed one command, your dog will jump and retrieve on the command to jump.

To retrieve over a jump, your dog has to go on faith since she probably will not be able to see where the dumbbell landed until after she jumps. When a dog retrieves an object she can't see, it is called a *blind retrieve*.

Your dog has to make two jumps. She should go out over the jump, pick up her dumbbell and return over the jump with it.

Relationship to Conformation

Jumping helps keep dogs in good, hard condition. Dogs with soft toplines, due to lack of musculature, often improve markedly after several weeks of jumping practice.

Equipment

Besides the lead and collar, you will need your dumbbell, a high jump, a twenty-five-foot light line, a ruler and a yardstick.

Obedience Regulations, your required reading, devotes its last few pages to how obedience jumps are constructed. The majority of exhibitors purchase their jumps already made. There are a vast array on the market, from the regulation show jumps to portable practice models. Your local kennel or obedience club should be able to help you acquire jumps, and they are also advertised in many dog magazines.

To determine the ultimate height that your dog will have to jump, you have to look it up in the *Obedience Regulations* because some breeds are required to jump one and one-quarter times their height at the withers and others must jump only one times their height. Section 10 of the regulations will tell you the requirement for your breed.

To measure your dog's height, place something flat and thin, like a ruler, across your dog's withers (the highest point of the shoulders, just behind the neck). Then put the end of a yardstick on the floor beside your dog and record where it meets the ruler. That's how tall your dog is.

TEACHING THE EXERCISE

Since your dog already knows how to retrieve, lessons begin without the dumbbell.

Teaching the Command

With your dog on a taut lead (as when you began teaching heeling), sit her at heel, facing the jump, about eight to ten feet from it. You are going to walk over the jump together, but she, not you, should be well centered. Move your jump to a different location every few days and keep it so low that both of you find it easy to walk over.

Without raising the jump, put your dog on lead on a sit-stay about three feet from the jump. Then walk to the other side, stand centered just a foot or two from the jump and give the jump command: "Mancha, over." Start moving backward when you are sure she will take the jump and spread your arms to receive her with a hug. No formal fronts yet. If necessary, use the line to guide her over the jump and toward you.

If your dog doesn't respond right away, pull her toward the jump to get her on her feet and praise enthusiastically. Do not give a second jump command.

Angle Jumping

When she has mastered walking over the jump on command, begin sitting your dog slightly off-center from the jump. Guide with the lead, if necessary.

Place your dumbbell about three feet on the other side of the low jump. Then line up with your dog on lead about three feet behind the jump.

When teaching angle retrieves over a low jump, guide your dog over the jump if she tries to cut around it.

Gradually increase the angle until she is sitting even with the jump standard and will take the jump on command, on lead, without your guidance.

Adding Height

Begin raising the jump two inches every few days until it reaches the lowest height where your dog has to jump rather than walk. Remain at that level and practice with your dog centered at first, then gradually increase the angle as before.

Introducing the Dumbbell

Lower the jump to walking height again and, with your dog on a six-foot lead, sit her only three feet from it and centered.

Command "Stay," step over the jump and place the dumbbell three feet on the other side of it (five feet for giant breeds). Return to your dog and command "Mancha, over, fetch." After about two weeks, drop the fetch command and use only your dog's name and "over." When you have to move forward to keep the lead slack for your dog to retrieve, move after she jumps.

If your dog does not retrieve, set up the collar, pinch her ear and keep the pressure on all the way to the dumbbell. As soon as she has the dumbbell in her mouth, whether she did it on her own or you had to correct her, begin backing up so that she will return over the jump. Guide her into a straight front, give your out command, take the dumbbell and praise her. Continue working at this height until your dog starts back to you over the jump without your having to back up or guide her. Then add distractions.

Angle Retrieves

When your dog is reliable with your most creative distractions, begin placing your dumbbell on the other side of the jump at an angle. Keep your dog close to the jump and on lead so that you can guide her. Gradually increase the angle until your dog can actually see the dumbbell on the other side of the jump and do not take her off lead until she masters severe angles, going and coming.

With your dog on a sit-stay, begin tossing the dumbbell at times instead of placing it. This transition usually goes smoothly. If she refuses, use the ear pinch. If she anticipates, correct the sit-stay, but not roughly.

Increasing the Jump Height

When your dog takes angles well over a low jump, begin increasing the height by two inches a week until you arrive at your dog's correct jump height. She will have to start farther back to get the momentum to jump, so use a twenty-five-foot light line and back up gradually until you are the required eight feet or more from the jump. Toss the dumbbell most of the time instead of placing it, but vary this a little. Remember to throw straight sometimes, but continue to practice angles that range from slight to extreme as you work at each new height. Invent new distractions for every level.

Don't send your dog every time. Sometimes leave her on the stay and walk out to retrieve the dumbbell yourself. Other times walk out, busy yourself examining the dumbbell, then put it back down, return to your dog and send her. Use the ear pinch correction for any refusal to jump or retrieve.

General Rules for Practice

- When running toward the jump, loosen the lead or line several feet before your dog jumps so that there is no tension on it to play havoc with her timing. Praise her as soon as she lands.
- When your dog is jumping angles on the longe or light line, arrange the line so that it doesn't get snagged by the jump standard.
- Don't take your dog off line until she can do angled retrieves with tempting distractions.
- If your dog tries to return around the jump off line, stay "Uh-uh" as you walk toward her. Take the tab and lead her back far enough so that she can get a running start at the jump.
- No matter how well your dog jumps, don't increase the height more than two inches per week.
- Once your dog is jumping full height, vary the height of the jump by lowering it at times so that your dog becomes conditioned to jump whatever height she sees.
- Move your own jump around frequently and take advantage of every opportunity to practice on someone else's jump. Disguise yours at times by draping a dark towel over it, hanging something on the standard or placing items on the ground beside it.
- Practice angles and distractions every time you train.

Common Errors of the Dog and Simple Corrections

Climbing the jump. Lower the jump. To build speed and confidence, put your dog on a longe line and start about eight feet from the jump. Command "Over," run with her and center your dog on the jump while you go around it. Be careful not to catch your lead or your arm on the standard.

When your dog has built more speed, try retrieves over the jump with lots of distractions and hope she will forget to jump or retrieve, get an ear pinch and concentrate on the job from then on. Gradually raise the jump.

Knocking the jump over. If your dog is hitting the jump because she is lazy, follow the same procedure as for climbing (above). If she simply isn't looking at the jump, try to slow her down. Don't run or throw a toy to get her to jump—just guide her by the collar.

If your dog isn't lazy or rushing the jump but still hits it hard enough to knock it over frequently, take her to the veterinarian for a checkup. She could have problems with her eyes or hips.

Ticking the jump. String thin wire tightly just barely (one-quarter inch) above the top board of the jump.

Failing to retrieve. Use the ear pinch.

Failing to jump going out, returning or both. Snub up the line and guide her over. When she reaches the other side, give an ear pinch. After she picks up her dumbbell, guide her back over the jump and praise her.

If she goes out over the jump and retrieves her dumbbell but tries to return around the jump, walk toward her saying "Uh-uh" as soon as you realize she isn't jumping. Then lead her back to a distance she can safely jump from.

Stopping dead in front of the jump. If this happens only occasionally in the early stages of training, take your dog by the collar, guide her far enough back from the jump so that she can get a running start, remove your hand and run with her. Center her while you either go over with her or around.

If it happens frequently, your dog lacks confidence. You probably raised the jump before she was ready or didn't proof her enough with distractions. Backtrack by lowering the jump to where she can walk over it. Then work your way back up slowly, with lots of distractions and lively praise.

IN THE RING

Responsibility of the Dog

- Sit-stay.
- Leave the handler on command to jump.
- Go over the jump on the way out.
- Pick up the dumbbell.
- Automatically come back over the jump while holding the dumbbell.
- Front holding the dumbbell.
- Release the dumbbell on handler's command.
- Finish on command.

Identical to retrieve on the flat, except that the dumbbell must be thrown at least eight feet beyond the jump or the judge will ask you to throw again. In addition:

- Know the proper jump height for your dog.
- Stand eight feet or more behind the jump.
- Politely refuse to send your dog over the jump if the footing is dangerous.
- Make a true enough toss so that when your dog returns after retrieving, the jump will be in her direct line of vision.

Common Handler Errors and Simple Corrections

Issuing an extra command or signal. Your dog must do every part of the exercise except the finish on one command.

Not having your hands at your sides.

Passing

Your dog will probably pass if she goes over the jump on one command, retrieves the dumbbell, brings it back over the jump and sits within reach—provided she does not climb the jump or knock it over. Major points are lost for dropping the dumbbell and picking it up to complete the exercise, or slightly touching the jump, but she may still pass.

The Australian Terriers, Ch. Beschutzer Fire of Kassander, UDT (left) and his dam, Ch. Beschutzer Mustic Blue Fire, UD,TDI (Therapy Dogs International), owned, trained and shown by Barbara Curtis. These two also point out that the aptitude for training, like physical appearance, is definitely inherited.

Anticipation and Hesitation

$\mathbf{F}$EW DOGS LEARN ANY EXERCISE without experiencing difficulty understanding exactly *when* you want them to do it. But questions of timing aren't limited to beginners. Even dogs who have performed an exercise well for many months may suddenly become overeager or plead ignorance for no apparent reason.

ANTICIPATION

During the first weeks of teaching an exercise some anticipation should be excused. When a previously reluctant dog tries to grab the dumbbell before she's been asked to, spit out the command and praise like crazy. Honest anticipation—when your dog thinks she knows what you want and just hurries to please, or when she concentrates so hard on a task that she forgets to wait—can be corrected with gentle techniques.

Include the following procedures early in your training program to prevent future problems:

- Frequently praise your dog before sending her on retrieves, jumps or any task she is likely to anticipate. Praising before commands will relieve anxiety about her ability to perform the next task, help her focus on what she is currently doing (even if it is just sitting) and encourage her to engage with you rather than act independently.

- Instead of issuing a command or signal at the normal time, fake out your dog by saying part of her name, coughing, bending your knees or, to proof signals, shrugging your shoulders or twisting your upper body. Praise right after every fake out so that she understands that waiting was the right decision.
- On practice run-throughs, with a friend playing judge, silently count to three before responding to the "judge's" "Forward," "Stand your dog," "Call your dog" or other commands your dog anticipates.
- Correct anticipation on new exercises by firmly and gently repositioning your dog with the lead or collar, not your hands. It often helps to praise her while you are restraining as she settles back in.
- Never repeat the stay command or give warnings like "Easy" or "No no." Talking will make your dog dependent on warnings and more anxious and convinced that something is wrong and you must really want her to perform. She will feel deprived in the same way that telling someone, "Whatever you do, don't touch this button," will pique curiosity and provoke button pushing.
- Avoid eye contact, touching and fumbling during corrections. Communicate with matter-of-fact, unemotional techniques.
- Don't correct a dog that lurches and then corrects herself, even if she fixed her mistake after realizing that she was in for a correction. As long as your dog wasn't distracted, praise her generously for catching her error.
- Correct seasoned or intense dogs with a quick, light jerk. If more than that is needed, it probably means your dog hasn't been proofed well enough around distractions and needs work on sneakaways to improve attention.

Your best bet for correcting even serious anticipation problems in advanced dogs is following the calm procedures above. Avoid extreme corrections like screaming, jerking severely or having "judges" repeat commands a zillion times in authoritative tones. These techniques may be successful in class but are likely to make the anticipator even more panicky in the long run. When faced with the stressful show atmosphere, she surely will not be relaxed enough to wait for your command.

HESITATION

When you give a command and your dog doesn't move, lurches forward but doesn't follow through or doesn't go in the right direction, don't be tempted to give her a break and start over by repeating the command. Since she doesn't understand your reasoning, she could become more confused over when the exercise starts and decide that sitting still, lurching forward or wandering around are all appropriate responses to your request.

Make your dog complete the exercise every time you give a command, even if a train went by or the lead accidentally tightened as she started on her way. Guide her gently and rather quickly if you feel her confusion is honest.

On new exercises where you are standing still and she must move, give your dog a few seconds to think the situation out. When all hope is lost, approach, take her collar and firmly guide her to complete the exercise.

Correct with more vigor if your dog is distracted or is advanced and has no good reason to be hesitant.

If you've made several corrections for hesitation to no avail, change exercises and come back later, or make the task simpler. For instance, if your dog didn't go out for articles, place a dumbbell in tall grass and send her. Correct with an ear pinch if she ignores your command since a Utility Dog certainly has no excuse for being hesitant about a retrieve on the flat.

Don't despair when your dog experiences problems with hesitation and anticipation. Instead, count your blessings. She is developing better comprehension and will end up more reliably trained than a dog who doesn't experiment with her options.

The Australlian Cattle Dog, Ch. Mikarin Red Viking, CD, U.-C.D., TT, HC, owned and trained by June Zuber is also a Hearing Alert Dog and holds the Dog World Award.

Broad Jump

Prerequisites

Your dog must be able to perform a reliable, formal Novice recall.

What's New?

Your dog's broad jump will be double her high jump, so if your dog high jumps twenty inches, she will broad jump forty inches. There are quite a few new moves in this exercise and some of them are yours, not your dog's.

Line up your dog on a sit-stay, eight feet or more behind the jump. On the judge's command, leave your dog, go to the right side of the jump anywhere between the first and last boards, and face the side of the jump with your toes about two feet from it. Send your dog on command and make a quarter turn to the right, in place, while she is in midair. Upon landing, your dog should automatically make a U-turn to the right and return to you in front position.

Some dogs ready themselves for the U-turn while still in midair. It is best if conformation dogs have a little less snap and not stress their bodies.

Relationship to Conformation

Improves muscle tone, particularly in the rear and the top of the back.

Equipment

The AKC's *Obedience Regulations* will tell you the distance your dog must jump, the number of boards you will need and how to build the jump if you are

Walk your dog over the hurdle until she jumps without hesitation. If your little dog is too tiny to start out jumping a whole broad jump board, elevate a two-, four- or six-inch-high-jump board.

handy. When you purchase a ready-made set of jumps, the broad jump will be included.

Before you start to train, purchase some chicken wire as wide as your broad jump and from ten to thirty inches long, depending upon the size of your dog. Training needs also include your lead, longe line, bar jump and toys. For tiny dogs, you may borrow a board from your high jump as explained in the following section.

TEACHING THE EXERCISE

For toy or very short-legged dogs, make a mini broad jump from a two-, four- or six-inch high-jump board. Angle it like a regular broad jump by placing something under the corners. Consider your dog's size and athletic ability to determine how small the beginning jump should be.

Dogs of normal size and build can start with the regulation boards. Use one for small dogs and two boards close together for medium or large dogs.

Introduce the broad jump the same way you did the high jump—with your dog beside you on a taut lead. Practice a few days or until she is no longer hesitant and doesn't try to go around it. If she decides to stop dead, just keep walking and don't even be concerned if she steps on the boards.

When walking over the jump becomes easy, stand eight feet from it, command "Over" and run over the jump with your dog.

Going it Alone

Place your dog on lead, on a sit-stay, about four feet from the jump. Holding the lead slack, leave her, walk to the side of the broad jump and stand two feet from the board(s) facing the side of the jump. Look at your dog as you give the over command in a cheery tone and begin running diagonally so as to meet her when she lands in front of the jump. Continue running with her for about eight feet, then back up several feet and have your dog come front.

Building Distance

To increase the distance of the jump, sit your dog farther back and switch to the longe line when necessary. Change to the regulation board for toy and short-legged dogs.

Fold your chicken wire in half and set it down, peak up, just between the first and second boards if your dog is using two or graduating to three boards. Little dogs need several sessions with the regulation board before a second board and the chicken wire are introduced. Arrange the wire somewhat higher than the jump boards to encourage your dog to make a high jumping arc. Later you can increase the height if your dog still needs more drive. An added bonus is that

Line your dog up on the left half of the jump, stand at the side and look straight ahead until you send her. The bar on the right half of the jump discourages cutting corners. The chicken wire pyramid in the center encourages height and discourages walking between the boards.

Look at your dog as you send her, then run to meet her.

Throw a toy when your dog takes her first step toward the jump. Gradually delay throwing it until your dog is in midair.

chicken wire also keeps your dog from walking on the ground between the jump boards.

Place the bar from the bar jump on the right corner of the broad jump to keep your dog from cutting corners; this may also help her to follow through and maintain her speed after landing. Do not practice fronts again until you reach the section titled "Adding the Front."

Start making your dog take the first step toward the jump without your having to run at the same time. Move after she does and meet her several feet in front of the jump to offer a toy and some play. If she does not move out on command, hold the lead tight enough so that when you move, she will receive a correction. Loosen it immediately so that you do not jerk her across the jump. Begin using distractions and sometimes return and praise your dog for staying instead of commanding her to jump every time.

When your dog starts toward the jump on command, throw a toy in front of the jump. Gradually toss the toy later and later until your dog is in midair before you throw it. Add distance gradually, no more than four inches a week and less for little dogs.

Adding the Front

Begin to condition the front about one-quarter of the time. Run out to your dog after she jumps, and when she slows down, take several steps directly backward and call her to front. The rest of the time alternate between throwing a toy and running out to meet your dog just to play with her. Continue practicing these variations on the longe line for two weeks before moving to the next step.

To teach your dog to turn and front after the jump while you turn in place, pivot while she is in midair and call her to front just as she lands. Give her the toy as soon as she sits in front. In the beginning you may need to reel her in and encourage her.

Do the pivot and front only one-third of the time. Otherwise, continue to motivate by either throwing a toy or running out to play.

Preventing Anticipation

Avoid anticipation by giving verbal praise instead of the jump command as you stand next to the jump, looking at your dog. If she lurches as you praise but settles back into a sit, continue praising. If she starts moving forward, return quickly and gently move her back into position. Then correct with an upward jerk. Try this a few times a week.

General Rules for Practice

- Always loosen the lead before your dog jumps.
- Do not increase to three boards until your dog has to jump forty-eight inches.

- If your dog will jump four boards at the show, practice that way only enough so that she won't be surprised by it in the ring. She will be less likely to walk through the jump when she sees less open space between the boards than she is accustomed to.
- Do not practice without props (bar, chicken wire) until your dog has perfected the exercise. Then do no more than two jumps a week without them.
- Go off line after your dog reliably jumps the full distance and returns to front with no prompting.

Common Errors of the Dog and Simple Corrections

Cutting across the jump. Place the bar from the bar jump across the right corner.

Walking through, touching or not clearing the jump. To encourage your dog to approach the jump with more speed and thrust, create a large arc of chicken wire and/or set up the bar jump in the middle of the broad jump. Make it no higher than half the distance of the broad jump.

Anticipating the jump. Review "Preventing Anticipation," above.

Failing to jump. If your dog is on lead or line, run as if you were going to meet her on the other side of the jump so that she gets jerked off the sit. If she is off lead, walk up to her collar and give a jerk to start her running toward the jump. Then put her back on line for several sessions.

Skipping the jump and going directly to you or going on the left side of the jump. Take your dog by the collar to a point where she can get a running start at the jump. Release the collar as soon as she is running toward the jump, but continue running beside her. For chronic problems, keep a bar jump standard at each side of the broad jump for two months.

Not returning directly to you. Walk up to your dog after she jumps and just before you expect her to meander. Grab her collar and jerk her toward you as you back up and praise. Remove your hand but continue backing and praising until both of you are in the proper position beside the jump.

IN THE RING

Responsibility of the Dog

- Sit-stay.
- Jump the broad jump on command.
- Automatically make a U-turn and return to front.
- Finish on command.

Responsibility of the Handler

- Position your dog the same distance from the jump that you practiced at home (at least eight feet).
- Stand with normal posture, hands at your sides, and give commands in your usual tone.
- Look at the same point (directly at your dog or somewhere above her head) that you do during practice.
- Position yourself in exactly the same area by the side of the jump where you stand at practice.
- Perform a right quarter turn, in place, while your dog is in the air.

Common Handler Errors and Simple Corrections

Using body English. Resist the strong tendency to lean toward your dog or over the jump while giving the command.

Passing

If your dog waits for the command to jump, clears the jump and returns close enough so that you can touch her without stretching, she will pass.

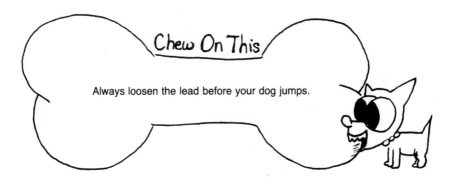

Chew On This

Always loosen the lead before your dog jumps.

Show Business: Open

Before You Enter

- Review "Show Business: Novice" (see page 101).
- Practice exercises around the jumps. When near a jump, some dogs lose their concentration and seem to wonder if jumping should be their top priority. Do recalls, retrieves on the flat and heeling patterns alongside, diagonally and in front of the jumps.
- Accustom your dog to jumping different-looking jumps. Although regulation jumps are made to certain standards, minor differences in construction could adversely affect her confidence. If possible, practice with jumps made of canvas, plastic, PVC and, of course, wood. Draping a sheet or towel over your jump or hanging a hat or jacket on the standard will also prepare your dog for any jump she may encounter.
- Introduce the stand for measurement by commanding your dog to stand and holding her head by the cheek or muzzle while someone measures her shoulder height with a yardstick. If she leans or shies away from the examiner, try the following:

    —Carry a stick if your dog isn't used to seeing you with a broom, shovel or pooper scooper. Before going to the next steps, let her see you with a yardstick often enough so that it becomes routine.

    —Approach your dog with a yardstick when she is on a sit-stay. If she becomes uneasy, move around her casually, keeping the stick at a

191

distance that makes her just a little edgy. To correct movement, first put the stick down, then jerk upon her collar. Gradually bring the stick closer until you can touch her shoulder with it.

—Excite your dog as you do for the dumbbell by tapping the measuring stick on the ground and moving it away. Then hold it horizontally about a foot away and give the fetch command. Use the ear pinch to correct.

—If your dog is excitable or shy, tell the person who is helping you by measuring her not to talk, make eye contact or touch her more than necessary. Correct movement quickly and silently as on the stand for examination.

—If your dog still leans away from the yardstick, ask the person playing judge to put it on her right side so that it will be between you and your dog.

At the Show

- Tell the steward your dog's jump heights when you pick up your arm-band.

When It's Your Turn

- Give the steward your dumbbell.
- Check the jump heights.
- Take your lead off and enter the ring when the judge or steward tells you to.
- Stand your dog for measurement upon entering the ring. You may touch your dog to position her and are encouraged to hold her head as you do when a conformation judge examines her. Thereafter you may touch only to praise, not to position.
- Beware of body English like leaning, nodding or jerking.

Dog Trainer's Depression

$\mathbf{F}$OR MOST OBEDIENCE ENTHUSIASTS, dog training is a hobby and hobbies are supposed to be fun. But if you have deluded yourself into thinking that every training session should be enjoyable and every show rewarding, it will be difficult to endure the tough times. Depression, to one degree or another, is a normal cycle in life and in dog training. Without the lows, the highs wouldn't feel so good—or as well earned.

REVIVING ENTHUSIASM

Psyching yourself up for training after a tense day at work and an aggravating drive home can be a major struggle. How can you revive your lost enthusiasm for training? The following suggestions should help.

Keep a training diary. You may think that you've devoted more time than you have or you may discover that your dog is making progress faster than you thought. Looking back over a diary will remind you how bad a problem was when you started and how far you have come. Some trainers are motivated to practice simply because if they don't, it becomes a matter of permanent record in their diary.

Meet with friends for training sessions. You can help each other set up equipment, work out problems and provide distractions. Besides, it's more fun and you are less likely to skip practice after scheduling it with others. The socialization is good for your dog's attitude too, and you are not likely to lose your cool after a frustrating problem while others are watching.

If you have no one to train with, hire a neighborhood youngster to help with distractions and equipment. Yes, you'll have to invest time training the kid, but your practice sessions will become more beneficial.

Get down to your dog's level and play with her, pet her or just sit close to her occasionally during the session. Rest for five minutes. When you resume training, you'll both be relaxed, refreshed and feel more like a team—guaranteed!

Don't set out to make a specific point in a given training session. An all-or-nothing attitude can send vibrations of frustration and tension straight down the lead, and those ingredients never produce good training rapport. If your dog doesn't learn the finish today, there is always tomorrow or the next day.

If getting started is your biggest problem, promise yourself you'll only review for five minutes and only your favorite exercises. When time is up, put your lead away if you want, but once you start, you are apt to enjoy it and continue.

Play your favorite music. You can't help but have fun listening to "Jail House Rock" or "On the Road Again," and music will enliven your movements. If a recording of a run-through or randomly called exercises would motivate you more, make a tape. Change it frequently to keep both of you sharp.

Review videos of teams you admire and of your and your dog's best work. It will help you visualize the performance you are striving for. Don't erase the videos of your really rotten run-throughs. Watch them when you need to be reminded of how far you've come.

PUTTING THE GLOW BACK IN THE SHOW

When humbling experiences or catty competitors make you start dreading competition, take charge of your show weekends by determining to give yourself a good time no matter how well you compete or how much others complain. The following plans and projects will at least keep you busy.

Go to dinner with friends after the show. Many exhibitors swear by this as the best remedy for a bruised ego and the perfect atmosphere for catching up on the latest gossip.

Bring a project to work on while you are waiting. Use your spare time at shows to read a book, write a letter or finish a drawing of your favorite dog. After all, how often do you have spare time at home?

Travel to shows with friends. Since you have to plan when to leave, where to stay and where to eat, it makes the day or weekend seem more festive.

Instigate a luncheon or an after-competition party, barbecue or luau for the next show. If you must, find something to celebrate—birthdays (dog or human), titles, weddings or big wins.

Choose optimistic company and conversation. Complainers and poor sportsmen with negative attitudes will dampen the most sunny spirit. Politely excuse yourself if you become a sore loser's target.

Remember that it isn't ever raining just on you. When ring conditions are bad, they are bad for the whole competition.

If nothing else helps, try taking a month off from training and involving yourself in a completely different dog activity like fieldwork, coursing, herding or agility. Help teach a class of novices. Attend a show without your dog and leisurely watch conformation and obedience. Spend several weeks interacting with and enjoying your dog simply as a pet owner.

One person's sacrifice is another's privilege. A match can be a social event or the obligation that kept you from finishing the yard work. You may be thankful you have the means to enjoy this pastime or resent the drain on your checkbook. Once you have decided that the sacrifices and investments you make for your sport are worth it, don't allow someone else's bad attitude to interfere with your fun.

OPEN:
Turning It Blue

Drop on Recall

T HE COMPETITIVE DOG must drop immediately, not sniff or hesitate before the drop, and should get up and return briskly when recalled.

PERFECTING THE FINE POINTS

Ironically, the best way to perfect this exercise is not to practice it as an exercise. Practice random drops in more challenging and spur-of-the-moment situations than your "Earning the Green" counterparts. Puddles, gravel, manure, plowed, overgrown and freshly cut fields, ice-covered or uncomfortably but not dangerously hot parking lots provide excellent testing grounds. Surprise your dog with a down command when she is playing with her pals, having an exhilarating romp in the park, in her kennel watching a loose dog wander the boundaries of her property or scavenging the kitchen floor while you are preparing dinner. Correct for creeping and sniffing as described in "Earning the Green" (see page 155).

When practicing formal drops:

- Drop your dog about 40 percent of the time, fake out your dog about 40 percent of the time and call her straight in as in Novice 20 percent of the time. Depending upon your dog, you may need to adjust these numbers.
- Vary the point where you drop your dog and the length of your recalls.

- Vary how long you keep your dog down before calling.
- Position the jumps in odd and common places in relation to your recall.

Continue practicing random drops. If your dog drops when she least expects to, the drop on recall will be simple by comparison.

MOTIVATION

Praise your beginning dog immediately after dropping or correcting, but vary your congratulations with the more experienced dog. Sometimes praise immediately; other times count to five first. In either case, break off with a big release and run away.

Problems

If your dog returns slowly after the drop, down her when she is feeling lazy, such as just after a nap or a long car ride. Walk about six feet away and call her. Correct only for walk-ins or if your normally fast dog approaches nonchalantly. Make the correction by walking up to her collar and giving one to three jerks as you back up and praise. Remove your hand, but continue walking backward quickly to see if your dog keeps up the pace. End with the sit in front and release with much motivation. Never practice more than two of these in a row and never more than once a day. The point is not to warm your dog up or worry her over the exercise. Worried dogs become tentative.

Even when lining up and practicing the drop formally (as in the ring), release and run away after most drops instead of calling your dog into a formal front.

Don't correct a tentative dog. When in doubt, give her a month practicing formal recalls. Sometimes throw out a toy after she sits in front and other times after she finishes.

If your dog starts to anticipate the drop, continue dropping her sometimes during practice anyway. More likely than not she really is trying to please. Put her in situations where she is likely to drop by mistake, then calmly and gently pull her in as described in "Earning the Green." That should teach her to wait for the command.

Return to dogs who don't drop promptly rather than calling them in.

PROOFING

Have someone call their dog as you are calling yours so that the dogs have to pass one another. Drop your dog when she is almost face-to-face with the other dog.

Before anything else, do a formal recall when you arrive at a new practice ground. Looking for places as close to people and dogs milling around as possible.

Walk seventy-five feet away from your dog and drop her when she first begins coming or after she reaches her peak speed.

HANDLING

Inflect your voice but keep your body still.

Chew On This

Beware of training in uncomfortable or dangerous places. Dogs lose faith in handlers who demand downs on too-hot pavement or send them over jumps when the landing is slippery.

Teach your dog to mark by throwing the dumbbell into tall grass and sending her while it is in midair. Gradually delay sending her.

Back up in "thinner thighs" position to get your dog to come into a straight sit.

Retrieve on the Flat

PERFECTING THE FINE POINTS

Encourage your dog to watch (mark) the dumbbell as it is thrown by sending her before it lands sometimes. Once she is watching and retrieving reliably, gradually delay your command more and more. If your dog can't find the dumbbell despite a frantic search, silently lead her to it by the collar but don't pinch unless she won't pick it up after being shown where it is.

Fetching Fabulous Fronts

Even dogs who do super fronts on straight recalls will probably have more difficulty with an object in their mouth. Maybe a dog requires the same extra concentration to sit straight *and* hold the dumbbell without mouthing as we need to pat our head and rub our stomach at the same time.

Dogs are more likely to touch you when fronting with something in their mouth. The most minor touch can cost a half point. Eliminate the problem by either teaching your dog to look up at you when she sits or to sit farther away.

The front box (see page 145) or lead can be used to teach your dog to sit farther away. For retrieving, design your front box with a thicker block in front of your feet, so that your dog has to sit farther out and can't touch. If you are going to use the lead instead, pull up and say "Sit" when your dog is at the proper distance.

To bring your dog's head up, drop food or a toy after you take the dumb-bell. As she is closing in on the front, assume the "thinner thighs" position (see page 145) and use your hand on the collar under her chin. Say "Head" and make your dog sit while your hand position on the collar forces her to look up. Then release your grip as you drop the toy.

Whichever method you choose, it may take months to pattern your dog into the new way of fronting with the dumbbell, so be patient.

If your dog needs more incentive, say "Head" a second before you expect her to bump you. If she touches, tap her under the jaw with just enough force to get her to lift her head. Then praise and back up to give her an opportunity to do it right. Soon she'll begin looking up, stopping farther away and sitting when you say "Head." If this method creates crooked sit problems, use the front box consistently.

PROOFING OPEN WHILE PREPARING FOR UTILITY

Practice extra-long tosses and throw into tall grass to teach your dog to mark the dumbbell when you throw and hunt for it when she loses sight of it. Understanding that she can never return without a dumbbell, no matter how difficult the retrieve, will ensure Open retrieves and is also necessary before teaching more intricate retrieving tasks in Utility. If you teach your dog to retrieve gloves, metal and leather articles and dowels, she will be familiar with the equipment when you begin Utility training. Start by holding the new object in your hand and telling her to fetch. Ear pinch to correct. When taking the object out of your hand is easy, place the item on the floor in front of her and then increase the distance gradually.

Even if you don't plan to continue into Utility, practice with other people's dumbbells and broken dumbbells. Remember, if your dumbbell breaks when you throw it, your dog is expected to return with a piece. Also, if you lose or forget your dumbbell, you will be glad that your dog is prepared to retrieve anything, even if her handler is absentminded.

Vary the length of time between throwing and sending. Some judges have you send immediately but others wait a few seconds.

HANDLING

Bull's-eye! Developing an accurate throw takes time and practice and is worth the effort even though it is not 100 percent reliable. Your dog must still be proofed against bad tosses, but accurate throws can make the difference between passing and failing, or the straight front that could determine who wins High in Trial.

If the retrieve on the flat is done close to the high jump and you are concerned about your dog returning over the jump, throw your dumbbell just beyond the twenty-foot marker. If the jump is in the center of the ring, throw as close to the ring barrier as possible.

Most dogs always turn in the same direction after picking up the dumbbell. If your dog is a right-paw turner, throw a little to the left (and vice versa) so she'll be lined up directly in front upon returning and can easily sit straight.

The English Cocker Spaniel, Ch. Mistral Apricot Brandy, CDX, owned and trained by Barbara O'Brien. *Janet Seltzer*

Retrieve over the High Jump

IF YOU have done your homework on fronts, finishes and the retrieve and jumping components, there is little to improve on for this exercise:

- Take your dog's turning direction into consideration when directing your tosses.
- Experiment with standing in different locations (you *or* her centered) and distances from the high jump to see if you get better fronts one way or the other. The farther back you stand, the longer your dog has to maneuver. That could be a plus or minus depending on her. A slow dog may benefit from your standing close so that she doesn't have time to lose points for slowing down after landing. A fast dog may need more distance to work on a straight front.
- Practice angled throws and use your front box to teach your dog to straighten out after landing. Be sure the box is far enough back not to interfere with her landing.
- Ring conditions may vary with poor lighting, amount of matting, uneven surfaces or mounds of fire ants, so prepare your dog for jumps in odd but safe places. Turn your high jump on a diagonal and practice heeling and flat retrieves close to your jumps.
- Remember to use ''fetch'' for your flat retrieve and ''over'' for the jump.

Line your dog up off-center so she has to go a little out of her way to jump.

The night before the trial.

208

Broad Jump

IF YOU ALLOW months of work with props (chicken wire and bar) to pattern your dog into the proper form, this exercise will be easy. But if you are anxious and always dabbling with how your dog will do without props, you will confuse her. The handler who is too lazy to remove and reset props will always come out ahead on this exercise.

PERFECTING THE FINE POINTS

When introducing the turn, position the front box in front of where your toes will be when you turn to face your dog. Drop a toy from your chin after she fronts to encourage a speedy return.

Continue to turn no more often than one out of three jumps and motivate the rest of the time.

Invisible Helpers

If you would like something less visible than the bar to discourage cutting corners, place a flat piece of two-feet by two-feet chicken wire on the right side of the end of your jump. Then, if your dog takes the wrong path back to you, she will land or walk on it. A second piece of wire can be used in front and to the right of you if your dog takes the scenic route rather than returning straight to you.

Speaking of visibility, lean a piece of Plexiglas, as long as your board and between six and twelve inches high (depending on the size of your dog), against the high end of the first board instead of the chicken wire pyramid. If you are trying to trick your dog into walking through, never allow her to see you handle the Plexiglas.

Permanent Props

If you wonder whether your dog is ready to jump without props, the answer is probably no because you are wondering. Even after your dog is showing and scoring well, use props and motivation most of the time when practicing the broad jump.

PROOFING

Practice leaving your dog to the right or left of the jump rather than centered so that she has to go a little out of her way to jump. Place boards in tall grass so that they don't appear to be elevated. Your dog will learn that "Over" means jump across the boards even though they are flat, and if you encounter a ring with tall grass, she will be ready.

HANDLING

When you go to the side of the jump, stand as far away from your dog as possible. That should encourage her to build momentum rather than twist as she jumps past you or turn to come back too quickly.

Try leaving your dog in front of the left half of the broad jump. If she jumps in a straight line she'll be able to make a smooth U-turn back to you and be positioned for a straight front.

When standing by the jump, look straight ahead or at the judge and turn to look at your dog just as you give the command.

Your dog is more likely to run toward the jump if you avoid staring at her as she approaches it.

Winning Without Warm-Ups

SOME OBEDIENCE TRAINERS go to great lengths to find a magic formula that will make their dog peak exactly when she walks into the ring. They experiment with how long their dog must be crated on the show grounds, how much time she should stand by the rings and how long and how intensely she should be exercised. Then they get lost or have a flat on the way to the show, or arrive on time to discover that half the class is absent, the other half had conflicts and they are first up instead of eleventh. So the best-laid plans often fizzle.

That is why it makes sense to teach your dog to give a quick, accurate response every time you give a command regardless of whether she is feeling lazy, bored, hyper or curious about her new surroundings. A dog that responds to commands immediately is always prepared for runoffs and also has an advantage in the breed ring. Turning on that expectant look or driving movement just one more time when she least wants to can win or lose the conformation class.

Issue commands like heel, sit, down, front and stay daily and be prepared to enforce them. If your dog is in the beginning stages of training and not ready to work off lead, practice in confined areas like the kitchen when you are preparing dinner or in the kennel when you are scooping. That way you won't need to put her in the mood by attaching a lead. Try giving commands when your dog doesn't expect them: when someone pulls into your driveway, when a neighbor walks past with his dog or when her favorite person comes home from school or work. Rousing her from a lazy sleep and asking her to heel well is a tall order and, when met, is worthy of lively play.

Are you worried that asking your dog to respond when she isn't in the right frame of mind is demanding too much of her and will turn her into a slave? Is she ever too sleepy to greet a guest or too relaxed to chase a rabbit? It is okay to expect her to have the same eager attitude about obedience and conformation.

UTILITY:
Earning the Green

Utility Work Ahead: Be Prepared

Taking directions from a distance and making multiple-choice decisions in new environments will be impossible for your dog unless she has learned to be attentive despite distractions. If she is still easily distracted, practice the Novice sections of "Turning It Blue."

Test your dog to see if she can retrieve a placed (not thrown) dumbbell, a dumbbell placed close by in low cover and one thrown far into low cover. If she has a problem, work on the retrieve on the flat in the "Turning It Blue" Open section.

Correct at the root of problems. For example, walking in shouldn't be corrected on the articles because it is a Novice recall problem, and sniffing the glove instead of picking it up is a retrieve, not a glove problem.

Utility Signal Exercise

Prerequisites

If your dog recently completed her CDX, she is ready to begin learning the signal exercise. If she's been on vacation or maternity leave, start by spending a few days reviewing heeling, first on and then off lead. Go over the recall, fronts and finishes and steady her stand-stay. Then practice random downs until she does them on the first command or signal without taking a few steps to think about it.

What's New?

This exercise is silent. You will use hand signals to perform a heeling pattern containing all the turns and changes of pace you learned in Novice as well as a stand, stay, down, sit, recall and finish. The judge will vocalize the heeling commands and the stand and will tell you when to leave your dog but will silently cue you to signal the drop, sit, recall and finish. Your dog will have to watch you carefully because the down, sit and come signals are given from across the ring.

New moves for your dog may include heeling into a stand, downing in place from a stand and sitting in place from a down. Your new moves are the hand signals and silence.

Relationship to Conformation

Performing an attentive stand-stay will give your dog an edge in the breed ring.

215

Equipment

You will need your collar and lead, plus the longe and light lines.

TEACHING THE EXERCISE

Before beginning the sit and down signals, teach your dog to respond to quiet verbal commands. With your dog sitting in heel position, say "Down" softly and don't say her name before the command. After she downs, softly command "Sit." Repeat and release. Use the lead to gently pull your dog up into a sit if she won't do it on her own, but jerk downward if she doesn't down. She is very familiar with the down by now, so she deserves a correction, but she may not have been taught to sit from a down, so guide her several times for a few days before correcting her.

Training Rules

- Make your signals as visual as possible.
- Begin close to your dog and do not allow creeping on the stand, sit or down.
- Gradually reduce the amount of help you give your dog as she shows understanding.
- It doesn't matter which hand(s) you use for the down, sit and recall signal, so decide which hand or which combination you prefer and remain consistent. You may only use one hand per signal, but you may change hands when you change signals. When teaching, hold the lead in one hand and signal with the other.
- Always return to correct your dog instead of repeating a signal, giving a verbal command or asking your dog to watch you. Give her a reason to watch (things are happening and if she doesn't watch she may miss something and be sorry). She will be more attentive with a reason than if she is watching because you commanded her to, in the same way that she watches out the window more intently when she is expecting you to come home than if someone simply commands her to look out the window.
- Expect good days and bad days during the learning phase and train accordingly. On bad days mix verbal commands with the signals. You might down your dog with a signal, then command "Sit." The familiarity of verbal commands may help get her out of a rut.
- If your dog resists being guided into position after a signal during the beginning teaching stages, softly issue a command without her name and correct for noncompliance, as during Novice training. After she does

signals without help, use distractions while you are still only one step away from her. When she looks away, signal and be ready to correct by stepping in, grabbing the lead and jerking her into position at the end of your signal.

- Prevent anticipation by sometimes shrugging your shoulders or wiggling a little before signaling. Praise your dog if she ignores it and guide her into the proper position if she doesn't. Don't flag your arms to fake her out because it is too easy to confuse this with an actual signal.
- Do the signals in sequence, but frequently hesitate, fake out by shrugging or return to praise between signals. After returning, either walk away to finish the sequence or release with praise and start a new sequence. If your dog is only having problems on the sit, consider leaving her in a down and practicing only the sit for a few sessions.
- Start with your dog on lead and graduate to the longe and then the light line as you move farther away. When your dog is reliable forty feet away under distractions, remove the line a few times a week.
- While practicing, sometimes ask family members or friends to act as distractions by standing behind and to the side of you and waving their arms like eager third-graders who want to lead the lunch line.
- Practice silent signals while others are practicing verbal commands, like "Down" and "Come," with their dogs.
- Work on different surfaces. Use wet grass, cold concrete and gravel but don't push it to the point of abuse. Bare bellies do not belong on hot sand or cement.
- Signal at different intervals. Count to two, three, four or five before doing your signal so that you know you are varying the length of time between them. This will condition your dog for judges who either hold signals or do them quickly.
- Practice in different locations with lively, noisy distractions.

Teaching the Signals

Heeling. Begin with the lead in your right hand in Novice training position. As you step off with your left foot, swing your left arm forward. If your dog doesn't naturally begin heeling, don't slow down. Softly command "Heel" (no name) and, if your dog still isn't in heel position, correct for lagging as in Novice and praise. The only difference between signal heeling and Novice or Open heeling is the use of a signal instead of a word to heel.

Stand. Use a sweeping motion of your right arm over your dog's eyes to her chest as your left hand touches her stifle to prevent sitting. If she still tries to sit or down, softly command "Stand." Gradually drop the command and the stifle touch. Stand erect beside her from one to five seconds (vary) before releasing her or commanding "Stay" and leaving.

Stay. Flash the palm of your left hand toward your dog in the same manner

The down signal. Step in as you signal to prevent creeping. Grab the lead on the down swing part of your signal to pull your dog down.

The sit signal. Step in to prevent forward movement and pull the lead upward as you signal. Praise by patting your dog's chest.

as for sit and down-stays and step off on your right foot. If your dog tries to follow, use the Novice stand corrections.

Down. Stand three feet from your dog and use a windmill-type hand signal. Step in and grab the lead on the down swing part of your signal to pull her down. If she braces, softly command "Down" (no name). If she still resists, correct with a downward jerk. Praise by scratching her rear thigh or above the tail to make her happy about the down position.

Sit. From three feet away, use an upward swing of your arm. Grab the lead on the way up as you step between your dog's feet. Praise by patting her chest.

Recall. From three feet in front with your dog in sit position, signal by bringing your arm out to your side at shoulder level. Sweep your palm into your chest as you grab the lead and move backward praising.

Finish. Use a sweeping signal of your left hand from in front of your dog's eyes to as far behind your leg as you can comfortably swing.

Common Errors of the Dog and Simple Corrections

Creeping. Correct on lead by stepping in to jerk your dog into place as soon as she attempts to move forward. If she only creeps toward you as you get farther from her, attach her line to something stationary behind her and leave her so that there is no slack but she can't feel that she is tied. When she tries to creep, the line will restrain her and you will correct with a jerk if she doesn't do the signal. This can also be done with a helper behind her holding the line.

Staying an inch or two off the ground on the down. Practice random drops on surfaces your dog doesn't like (wet, cold, gravel) and correct her by running in and using a downward jerk (two-handed for strong dogs). When your dog drops on all surfaces but still refuses to drop all the way on the signal, run in to administer the jerk. Frequently return and praise your dog after she drops by petting her thigh to relax her. Also try rubbing her tummy.

Not going into an erect sit. A dog who only comes up partway is usually very submissive. Return frequently to pet her chest. With confidence, she will straighten up. If she likes to play, toss a toy at her after she sits, just as you release her.

Missing signals. Run in to give a jerk down for down, up for sit or horizontal as you back up and praise for the recall. If your dog is on line, jerk in on the recall.

Walking forward on the stand or not remaining standing. Return to give a horizontal jerk and stifle touch. If this is a frequent problem, leave and return after five, ten or fifteen paces (vary) and give praise. Then leave again to give signals.

Note: All the heeling errors described in the Novice and Open and Novice recall sections apply to the signal exercise as well.

IN THE RING

Responsibility of the Dog

- Perform a complete heeling pattern on silent signals.
- Walk into a stand on signal.
- Stand-stay while the handler leaves.
- Obey handler's signals from a distance for down, sit and come.
- Finish on signal.

Responsibility of the Handler

Responsibilities during the Novice and Open heel free and the Novice recall apply. In addition:

- Give clear signals and bend when signaling a little dog to heel.
- Give the heel signal immediately before you move out.
- Don't say a word. If you have lost your dog's attention while heeling, this one is a judgment call. A verbal command to heel probably won't fail you, but a verbal command for stand, down, sit or come will.
- Think. If your dog looked toward a sudden noise for a second, wait a second (but not five seconds) before giving your signal.

Common Handler Errors and Simple Corrections

Handler errors from the Novice and Open heel free and the Novice recall apply. In addition:

Giving sloppy signals or signaling too fast. The signals take the place of a verbal command. You wouldn't mumble commands to your dog in the ring so don't blur your signals. Do them exactly as you practiced at home.

Moving out an instant before giving the signal to heel. Have a friend watch you. Most people don't realize that they do this and wonder why their dog always has a lagging start.

Holding signals too long. What constitutes "too long" is up to the judge. It usually results in points off but could be cause for failure if too pronounced.

Using body English with signals.

Passing

If your dog heels reasonably well and responds to your first signal to stand, stay, down, sit and come, she will probably pass. Slow responses and moving forward a little bit on the signals will cause her to lose points. Moving forward considerably on the stand, down or sit will keep your dog from qualifying.

Scent Discrimination

Prerequisites

When your dog is solid on the retrieve on the flat, she is ready to learn scent discrimination.

What's New?

Your dog will be required to do a half turn in place (pivot), either left or right.

Picking up an article that is already lying on the ground is new because your dog is used to seeing articles thrown in the ring. The dumbbells are also different since they are made of leather and of metal.

The object of the exercise is scent discrimination. Nine dumbbells of metal and leather will be on the ground and you will have touched one of them. Your dog has to find and retrieve the article you touched. This must be done two times: once for the metal and once for the leather.

Watch the Utility class at the show before entering. Several procedures are new, and since this is Utility, the judge doesn't expect to have to guide you every step of the way. Your *Obedience Regulations* booklet tells what to expect but doesn't follow a step-by-step progression. The order of events is:

1. Before your articles are laid out, two of them will probably be placed on the table or chair behind you. In rare instances, the judge will tell you to leave your dog and pick two from the pile.

2. You and your dog may watch the articles being laid out. They will be placed twenty feet or more from you and about six inches apart.
3. After your articles are laid out, turn your back to them with your dog sitting at heel.
4. Pick up and scent the article you want your dog to work first.
5. The judge will say, "Are you ready?" and the exercise begins as you place the article you just scented on his clipboard.
6. While you and your dog remain facing away from the ring, the judge will place (without touching it) the article you scented somewhere among the other articles.
7. The judge will command "Send your dog," and you will:
   a. Allow your dog to sniff the palm of one of your hands (optional).
   b. Tell your dog to heel and make a half turn in place either right or left. Your dog should pivot and sit at heel.
   c. Give the command to find and retrieve the correct article.
   d. Stand in place, hands at your sides, while your dog goes to the pile of articles, chooses one and returns to front.
   e. As in Open retrieving, the judge will tell you to take the article and to finish.
   f. When the exercise is finished, you and your dog will turn your backs to the pile, and you will start scenting the second article. From there on, go back to step 5 and follow through with the second article.

Relationship to Conformation

The scent discrimination exercise has no bearing on anything a dog is required to do in the breed ring.

Equipment

Bring your articles to the ring. A complete set of ten articles includes five metal ones, all alike and the correct size for your dog, and five similar leather articles. While you are allowed to create your own articles as specified in the regulations, almost no one bothers. Ready-made articles are sold at many obedience trials and are advertised in dog magazines. When ordering, keep in mind that scent article size relates to dumbbell size. Articles come with single, double and triple bars, and they all work fine, so make your own choice. Many obedience exhibitors have two sets and alternate when practicing. You can keep one set for "show" by using it once for every three times you use your "practice" set.

You will need something to carry your articles in. Cases especially made for this purpose are available, and people also create carriers made of everything from wire to wicker.

To teach this exercise you will need:

- an ordinary pair of tongs for handling the articles without getting your scent on them.
- lead and light line.
- lightweight string.
- a practice area where there is a stationary object such as a post or tree.
- a pen or pencil in your pocket.

Article Care

Get your dog accustomed to doing this exercise while you have the scent of whatever you happen to be around—soap, bait, other dogs—or when you get to the show, you won't be able to eat and will spend the day worrying about what you touch.

While you would never want to make this exercise more difficult by touching your articles within twenty-four hours of the show, dogs are really much better at scent, once they understand it, than we give them credit for. They can determine the article with the "hot" (recent) scent from those scented a few hours earlier. But why push it? Keep your hands off them.

TEACHING THE EXERCISE

Introducing the Articles

Begin with your dog sitting at heel, on lead. Command "Fetch," and put the metal article in her mouth. Cup your hand around her muzzle for a few seconds, give your command to release the article, take it and praise. Repeat with the leather article. Practice until your dog will hold each article without mouthing it and without your hands near her muzzle. Take it after ten seconds. If she drops it before you take it, use the ear pinch.

The next step is to get her to reach for the article in your hand; this is followed by getting her to pick it up from the ground after you place it. This is taught like the retrieve on the flat, but you will be able to speed through the steps since your dog already knows how to retrieve. Some dogs are less than thrilled by the feel of metal in their mouth and may need a few corrections.

Early Scenting

Allow your dog to see you half-hide an article one lead length away under leaves or straw, in tall grass or half under the end of a throw rug. Give scent by putting your right palm in front of her nose and saying, "Find it" or "Find mine." Alternate metal and leather.

Gradually hide more and more of the article and eventually stop making where you are placing it obvious to your dog. Use the ear pinch correction if she

If your dog tries to retrieve the unscented article, it will automatically be pulled out of her mouth when she reaches the end of the string.

If your dog stands still holding the wrong article, or if she makes a mistake when the articles are no longer tied down, flip the unscented article out of her mouth with a pen.

doesn't try to find it. If she tries but isn't successful, guide her all the way to the article on a tight collar. Stick with this step until your dog searches for hidden articles until she finds them.

There Are Strings Attached

A set of scent discrimination articles usually includes six of leather and six of metal even though only five of each type are used in the ring, the sixth being a "spare." In the instruction that follows, all the articles in the set are used.

Tie a two-foot string to three of your metal and three of your leather articles. Tie a four-inch string (two-inch if you have a tiny toy) to your remaining three metal and leather articles. It is important that you attach the strings at least twenty-four hours before you practice so that the wrong articles will not have strong scent on them when you begin teaching.

The articles that have two-foot strings will be tied to a stationary object. Do not scent them because they are supposed to be the "wrong" articles. Since they are tied, when your dog tries to bring one back by mistake, it will be pulled out of her mouth.

The articles on the short strings will be your scented articles. The reason for three of each is so you can alternate articles during practice instead of letting your dog get used to the same article every time. The strings are attached so that the scented article will look the same as the tied articles, and the string is short so that your dog will not step on it while carrying the article.

Early Scent Discrimination Exercises

Pick up one metal article by its long string (without touching the article) and tie it to a stationary object. Then scent a short-stringed metal article and place it about six inches from the tied one. To scent the article, hold the dowel(s) firmly in your hands and count to twenty slowly.

From about six feet away, face the articles with your dog on lead, give scent with your right palm and use your command for finding an article. If your dog picks up the right one, reel her in and praise her. If she picks up the wrong one and tries to come in, it will be pulled out of her mouth. When that happens, say and do nothing and hope she goes back and tries again with the correct one. If she quits working and appears to have no intention of trying again, or if she continually paws the article, guide her to the right one. Don't ear pinch unless she actually balks at picking up the correct article after you point it out to her. She does not understand the exercise yet and it may be some time before she realizes why one article is correct and the rest are not. As long as she is trying, guide—don't correct.

If your dog picks up the wrong article and stands still, holding it in her mouth, flip it out with your handy pen or pencil. Then guide her all the way to the right article so she can't make a detour and grab a wrong one again on that try. Never take the incorrect article from her mouth. Once you handle it, you have accepted it as the correct one.

Practice the same procedure at a different time using the leather articles.

Do not rush to add more articles. Your dog knows how to scent—all dogs do—but she has to learn the concept. Up until this exercise, she was praised for bringing back a dumbbell. Now she has to bring back a particular dumbbell. It won't take her long to realize that, but it may take time for her to figure out what makes a certain one the right one. You will know when she understands. It will be obvious in her eyes and her attitude.

When your dog picks up the correct metal and leather articles on every try three days in a row, begin adding easy distractions like another person moving around nearby or someone walking a dog near the article pile. As soon as she ignores them, add one tied article of each type, also six inches from the others, but don't combine the two materials yet. When she is reliable with two tied down, go to three. Once your dog can discriminate between a group of four (three tied and the scented one), with difficult distractions like people and dogs sitting on the ground near the articles, it is time to combine materials.

Combining Materials

When you begin combining metal and leather, start with one of each tied down and scent a short-stringed metal article. If your dog is successful, do a leather. Once your dog correctly scents both materials once, even if it is on the first try, go to a different exercise and come back to scenting later.

Work up slowly, adding one tied article at a time every few days and alternating materials. Begin adding distance too, and switch your lead for a line.

Turning Around

In the ring, your dog will have to pivot in place before you send her to find the article. Practice this move separately so that your dog becomes very familiar with it before you add it to the scent exercise.

Although your dog may turn in either direction to face the articles, we recommend an about-turn to the right. To teach it, command ''Around,'' turn in place 180 degrees to the right and halt. If your dog does not sit, correct with an upward jerk. Jump ahead if she doesn't move with you and come to a stop gradually.

When adding the around to the scent exercise, give scent first. Then command ''Around'' and turn in place to face the articles. Hesitate varying amounts of time before sending your dog to the articles. Sometimes praise, leave, return and then send.

Removing the Strings

When your dog successfully works five articles (four tied down) and seems to have gained confidence, stop tying the unscented articles. If she picks up the first article she sees or any wrong article, wait a second to see if she will realize her mistake and drop it. If she starts walking back with the incorrect article, walk into her and flip the article out of her mouth with a pen. Then guide her to the correct article.

When your dog is scenting well, continue adding articles, one every few days and gradually increase the distance to twenty feet. If she begins to have problems (two mistakes), reduce the number of articles and the distance.

General Rules for Practice

- Always scent the same material first (we recommend metal).
- When doing metal and leather together, do only one of each correctly before moving on to a different exercise.
- If your dog picks up the right article but is hesitant about bringing it back, don't coax her in with your voice. She will become dependent on it and it will be hard to wean her off. Instead, back up and reel in the line. If she drops the article on the way in and doesn't pick it up herself, pinch or guide her to it and continue backing up. You will have to read your own dog to know if you should pinch (balking) or guide (confused). Be miserly with corrections on this exercise. A dog who has become afraid to pick up any article at all is much harder to train than one who is simply making mistakes.
- As soon as your dog is reliable with just one article tied, begin inventing distractions. Make them harder as you go along and keep strings on the articles until your dog works despite your best creative efforts.
- When your dog has been doing articles successfully in various locations, always goes directly to the pile and doesn't try to avoid corrections, you no longer need to use the line. If she regresses (two mistakes), reattach it.

IN THE RING

Responsibility of the Dog

- Sit-stay at heel.
- About-turn or left U-turn in place.
- Go out on command and find the scented article.
- Return to front holding the article.
- Release article on command.
- Finish on command.

Responsibility of the Handler

- Walk your dog to the ring on a familiar lead she is used to smelling on your hands.
- Don't touch your articles for twenty-four hours before showing.

- Scent the designated articles the same way you do at home and try to smell the same way you normally do. Don't use a new perfume or after-shave and don't handle raw onions or garlic on the day you are going in the ring.
- If you give your dog your open palm to scent, do it before you turn to face the articles.
- Perform a clean pivot in place without excessive movement.
- Keep your hands at your sides while your dog works.
- Look at the same place you look at during practice while your dog returns with an article. If you normally look over her head and suddenly stare directly at her, she may lose confidence in her decision and drop the article.

Common Handler Errors and Simple Corrections

Overscenting the article. Rub it lightly with both hands, then hold it tightly in both hands for several seconds. That should be just right. Rubbing hard and long can make the scent strong enough to be uncomfortable to a dog.

Making a sloppy pivot. Practice pivoting several times without your dog once you decide which direction is best for her.

Issuing double commands. Beware of leaning forward as you send your dog.

Passing

If your dog goes out to the articles on your first command, finds the right one, brings it back far enough so that you can easily reach it and allows you to have it, she will probably pass. Of course, she has to do it twice. Stomping and fumbling articles loses points, as does jumping a jump and staring blankly at the articles before and in the middle of working them.

Directed Retrieve

Prerequisites

Your dog must be able to perform a reliable retrieve on the flat.

What's New?

You already learned to pivot in one direction for the scent discrimination exercise. For this one, you and your dog should know how to turn in place in either direction.

Retrieving an object by following a directional signal is new to your dog. Her act of watching your signal and looking beyond it to see the object is often called *marking*.

Picking up a soft, thin object is new. Your dog is used to solid objects with convenient bars in the middle.

Ring procedure: Following scent discrimination, go to a point even with and midway between the high and the bar jump. Face the end of the ring where you entered, with your dog sitting at heel. The gloves will be placed at the end of the ring while you are facing away. One glove will be laid in each corner and one in the middle. Facing them, they are designated 1, 2 and 3, reading from left to right.

The judge's command will be "One," "Two" or "Three" to tell you which glove your dog is to retrieve. Some judges may help you by pointing toward the glove, but many won't. Use your pivot command, face the correct glove and bend to show your dog a directional signal with your left hand as you give the retrieve command. Straighten up with your hands at your sides while your dog retrieves. From there on the judge's commands will be "Take it" and "Finish," as in an ordinary retrieve.

Relationship to Conformation

The directed retrieve exercise has no bearing on anything a dog is required to do in the breed ring.

Equipment

Obtain six white or nearly all-white cotton work gloves, although you will only take three of them to the ring. Try to get a small size for your tiny dog or she may step on her glove while carrying it.

Wash your gloves before a show and crumple them so they dry wrinkled. When they don't lie quite flat, they are easier for your dog to see. After they dry, have your dog retrieve each of them at least one time before you use them at a show.

When training, you will also need your lead and longe and light lines.

TEACHING THE EXERCISE

There are two parts to this exercise, and you can work on them during the same practice session as long as you don't combine them until your dog is ready.

Pivots

The word *pivot* sounds graceful enough to activate the footwork gremlins, but they won't have the opportunity to trip you up. Forget dancing-school spins. It is okay to use three or four tiny steps to complete your turn because, as long as you remain in place, it is still a pivot.

Start and end every pivot with your right foot. It doesn't matter what you do in between as long as you don't move out of place. Turn right for glove number 1 and left for number 3. You may go in either direction for number 2, but left is often safer. If your dog underturns on a left U, it is easier to block her vision of glove number 3 than it is to grab her attention away from glove number 1 if she underturns a right about-turn. Mark a spot on the floor and practice pivoting to each glove without your dog until you know how you will do it in the ring.

Use different words for each turn: "one," "two" and "three," or "right," "left" and "center" work fine.

The "Jackie Gleason left turn" (see Novice heeling, page 78) works well to teach medium and large dogs to make left U-turns. For little dogs, practice

Pluck out a handful of grass and place your glove in the bare spot. Signal with your whole arm and send your dog when she is looking in the right direction.

making a left turn every few steps while heeling and keep taking fewer and fewer steps before turning left. Soon you will be making left circles in place, and turns in place are pivots.

The right pivot is easier because your dog will step forward rather than backward. She only has to follow your left leg, so teach it like a heeling movement. If your dog makes a sloppy turn in either direction, use the same corrections used for heeling.

The Signal and Command

To signal direction, bend down so that your shoulder is close to your dog's eye level and extend your left arm as far as possible in the direction of the article but do not move your feet. Give the retrieve command just after your arm motion stops so that your dog can mark while your arm is in motion. Any hesitation between your arm stopping and your voice starting will fail your dog.

After your dog sees you place a glove on the ground, take her a lead length away and send her to fetch it. Practice retrieving easily visible, placed gloves until your dog retrieves quickly on command without mouthing, playing or fooling around. Begin with your gloves folded so that they will be easier to pick up and less appealing to shake. If she shakes them anyway, say "Uh-uh" quietly. If she persists, place pebbles or small fishing sinkers in the fingers and close the gloves with a rubber band.

Hide and Fetch

Place six gloves in different visible locations around your practice area. With your dog on lead, position her four feet from one of the gloves, signal and command "Fetch." Then practice a different exercise before you line your dog up for another glove. Repeat the procedure until all your gloves have been retrieved.

After two or three days of having your dog retrieve gloves in sight, begin hiding them. If you are outside, pluck out some grass and place your glove in the bare spot. On blacktop, use a brown glove. If you are working on mats or rugs, place the gloves partially under them. Work on lead, one glove at a time, with the signal and fetch command, just as you did with the visible gloves.

Combing Pivot and Retrieve

When your dog reliably retrieves hidden gloves from a lead length away, place two easily visible white gloves in the number 1 and 3 positions, also only a lead length away. Have your dog sit at heel, facing away from the gloves. Say her name and the pivot command ("Mancha, three"), and turn to face the glove. Make your signal deliberate, and be sure your dog sees it before you send her. If she isn't watching you, sneak away silently. When your dog understands the exercise and is doing well, add a glove in the number 2 position. Resist the temptation to ever practice more than one glove retrieve at a time and you may avoid some "go-out" problems later.

Distance and Direction

As your dog progresses, gradually increase to longe line distance, and finally to the light line. When your dog is 95 percent reliable and always returns, try it off lead sometimes. If regression occurs, go back on line.

Practice at various distances to be ready for variation in ring size and shape.

Sometimes underturn or overturn on purpose and send your dog to one glove when she is facing another.

General Rules for the Directed Retrieve

- Always move the gloves after a correction. By varying the presentation, your dog learns to take directions rather than memorize location.
- Use people, other dogs, strange places and noise as distractions, but don't lay treats or toys on the ground near the gloves.
- Use heeling corrections to shape up pivots.
- Do not always send your dog after you give the directional signal. Sometimes praise her for watching and heel off.
- Use sneakaways to insist that your dog watch you and not look toward the gloves until you signal. That way when you do signal, she will be less likely to be aware that there are other gloves out there.

Common Errors of the Dog and Simple Corrections

Veering off to the wrong glove. Snub up the line to stop her, grab her collar and bring her back to the path she should have taken. Then guide her to the glove with one hand close to her collar and the other holding the signal.

Refusing to retrieve. Snub up the lead and do an ear pinch with your right hand while your left arm continues to signal.

IN THE RING

Responsibility of the Dog

- Sit at heel.
- Pivot and sit at heel facing the proper glove.
- Watch (mark) the directional signal.
- Retrieve the correct glove on command.
- Front automatically and release the glove on command.
- Finish on command.

Responsibility of the Handler

- While watching the pattern before your turn, make a mental note of where the gloves are placed so that you can pivot to exactly the correct angle.
- Bend so that your hand is at your dog's eye level when giving direction, but don't move your feet or touch your dog.
- Make your signal clear by keeping your arm rigid and your fingers together so that your hand points toward the glove like an arrow.
- Give the vocal retrieve command when you complete the directional signal. Be careful not to jerk your arm or it will be considered a double command.
- After sending your dog, straighten up and stand naturally with your arms at your sides.

Common Handler Errors and Simple Corrections

Not turning in place. Practice pivots without your dog.

Excessive signaling while turning to face the glove.

Not pivoting to enough of an angle to line up well for the one or three gloves.

Overpivoting. Beware of turning too far. It looks like cheating and judges watch for it and take off points accordingly.

Repositioning the dog after the pivot and sit. If your dog is in a sloppy sit and facing halfway between two gloves, give a clear directional signal, send her and hope for the best. Jiggling around to realign her before signaling will make you fail the exercise.

Kneeling on the floor to signal a tiny dog. You may bend as far as necessary, but kneeling with one knee on the floor as you may do in the breed ring is not permitted. You may bend both knees to get down to Chihuahua or Yorkie eye level.

Going blank over which gloves "1" and "3" are. A nervous disorder, this occurs just as the judge gives the command. It passes in an instant, but it feels like longer. You may try to make up for your hesitation by doing a "stage-fright spin" instead of a deliberate pivot. That confuses your dog, who ends up sitting angled toward the wrong glove. So, if you are prone to nerves, wear light-colored shoes and pencil a "1" on the right shoe and a "3" on the left, just large enough for you to see easily. When the judge says the number, look at your shoes and make your turn.

Passing

If your dog waits for you to send her, goes directly to the correct glove and brings it back to within your reach, she will pass. If she checks out another glove before deciding upon the correct one, she won't qualify.

Moving Stand and Examination

Prerequisites

Your dog should already know the stand from the signal exercise, the Novice stand for examination and the recall.

What's New?

Unlike the signal exercise, where you stop with your dog, this time you will keep moving while your dog stops.

Although your dog is used to a thorough examination from the breed ring, you will be about twelve feet from her during this one so she won't have your reassuring presence. Also, the rules dictate that the judge will approach from the front, but an occasional judge approaches from an angle between the side and the rear.

This is the only exercise where your dog does a recall directly to heel position without a front.

Relationship to Conformation

Once your dog masters this exercise, you can show off in the breed ring by stacking her and walking to the end of your loosely held lead while the judge

Turn toward your dog and use your right hand on her chest to stop forward movement as your left hand touches her stifle to remind her to stand.

When teaching the moving stand, command and signal as you pivot in front of your dog and touch her chest and stifle.

Stand next to a barrier when teaching the call to heel. Use your signaling hand to pull your dog through the alley, if necessary.

examines her with no interference from you. It can also be impressively used at the end of the gaiting pattern.

Equipment

You will need your dog's collar, lead and light line.

TEACHING THE EXERCISE

Separate this exercise into three parts: stand, examination and call to heel. It is okay to work on all three parts during the same practice session, but don't put them together until your dog knows each part well.

The Stand

With your dog sitting at heel, on lead, and the lead in your left hand, begin heeling. Go straight ahead between eight and twelve feet, turn your body sideways toward your dog's shoulder and give the same signal to stand that you use during the signal exercise. Command either "Stand" or "Stay," whichever works best on your dog, and lightly touch her stifle with your left hand. Back away as soon as she is steady. Gradually discontinue the stifle touch and slow down less and less when giving the signal until you can put her on a stand-stay and move on with no hesitation. When returning, go directly to heel position without going around your dog, then praise and release.

The Examination

Stand your dog, give the stay command and signal, drop the lead and examine her. Run your hands down her legs, cup her head, tickle behind her ears and under her chin and pat her chest. Bend down beside her to run your hands down her front and rear legs, rub her belly and stroke her back from head to tail. Go behind her and stroke from the top of her withers down her shoulders and front legs. Feel under her chest and tuck-up, lift or handle her tail and run your hands from her hips down her back legs. When you are finished, stand straight by her side, then praise and release.

Ask other people to examine your dog thoroughly while you stand several feet in front of her holding a slack lead or line. When she is steady, remove the lead.

The Call to Heel

With your dog on lead and just walking casually or standing around, call her to heel. Use the verbal command and a sweeping finish signal as your left hand meets the lead and smoothly pulls it to guide her. If your dog doesn't walk back far enough, use a barricade on your left side as you did when first teaching the finish. Gradually remove the lead guidance and, eventually, the lead.

Combining Components

On lead, heel your dog into the stand and continue walking until you are six feet away. Wait several seconds, return and examine her lightly and silently. Go back out to the end of the lead, face your dog and call her to heel.

If your dog is tentative and slow on the call to heel, be patient. After she becomes comfortable with the exercise, her speed will probably increase. If it doesn't, or if she is extremely slow, pull her with steady tension on the lead and be careful not to jerk. The stress of a correction may make her want to return to the comfort of the familiar—in this case, a front.

When your dog seems secure with the exercise, put her on a long line, have people examine her and work up to thorough examinations with you twelve feet away. Have the "judges" approach from the side or an angle near the rear sometimes. Use distractions and practice in different places.

General Rules for Practice

- Always examine or have someone else examine your dog before calling her.
- To separate this exercise from the signal exercise, always use a verbal command to heel and heel in a straight line (no heeling pattern) before standing your dog.

Common Errors of the Dog and Simple Corrections

Every error that can be made on this exercise has already been covered in Novice heeling, the stand for examination and "The Finish" portion of the Novice recall.

IN THE RING

Responsibility of the Dog

- Heel into a stand-stay while you keep walking.
- Stand for a thorough examination, similar to those given in the breed ring, except that teeth and testicles will be excluded.
- Return directly to heel position on command.

Responsibility of the Handler

- Do not pause or stop when giving your dog the command and signal to stay.
- When you turn to face your dog on the judge's command, stand naturally with your arms at your sides.
- Call your dog to heel with a clear verbal command. You may also give a finish signal.

Common Handler Errors and Simple Corrections

Those heeling and recall errors described in the Novice section also pertain to this exercise.

Altering your normal heeling speed to prepare for the stand.

Passing

If your dog stops on command, remains standing with a pleasant or neutral attitude during the examination and returns within easy reach when you call her in, she should pass. Most points are lost for slight foot movement, slow response to return and poor finishes.

The Vizsla, Ch. Anderson's Golden Rebel, UD, SH, VC, owned by Nancy Anderson, is yet another example of a Sporting dog that has distinguished himself in conformation competition, obedience trials and as a gun dog. He is a senior hunter and his versatility certificate comes from the Vizsla Club of America. *Chet Anderson*

Directed Jumping

Prerequisites

A dog that is able to perform the Open retrieve over the high jump, will search for a hard-to-find dumbbell and is in good physical condition is ready to learn this exercise.

What's New?

The "go-out" with its distant sit is new, and some contend that the AKC made it part of the final exercise just to test how much we really want that UD title. On command and/or signal, your dog should run away from you in a relatively straight line between the two jumps and turn and sit facing you on command. The truth is, dogs don't understand the straight line concept and have trouble learning to run to the other end of the ring without veering. Some tend to go where they found the glove (if yours was number 2, it is your lucky day). Others arc when running or make a wide turn when stopping, which places them near a corner of the ring, far from one of the jumps.

The jumps will be about twenty feet from you, and your dog must go ten feet beyond them to pass. Twenty feet is ideal. So is sitting at the far end of the ring exactly in line with you.

Train your dog to take the correct directional jump signal from even the most distant corners of the ring. That way, no matter how crooked her go-out, provided it is ten feet or more past the jumps, she will still pass.

On the judge's command, "Send your dog," give a verbal and/or hand signal for your dog to leave. When she gets far enough, stop her by calling her name and commanding "Sit." Ideally she will turn, face you, sit and watch for your directional signal.

The judge's next command will be "Bar" or "High." Give your dog a verbal command to jump while using your arm to signal which hurdle. While she is in midair, turn in place so that you are facing her as she returns to sit in front. The exercise ends with a finish. Then you and your dog reposition yourselves facing straight ahead to repeat the exercise using the other jump.

Relationship to Conformation

The directed jumping exercise has no bearing on anything a dog is required to do in the breed ring.

Equipment

You will need your high jump from the Open exercises and a bar jump. The bar jump specifications are given in the *Obedience Regulations,* but if you purchased a ready-made set of jumps, you already own one. In the ring both jumps will be set at the same height your dog jumped in Open. They will be side by side, but about eighteen to twenty feet apart and around twenty feet from you.

You also need two or three dowels, some squares of "stick-on" Velcro and a white baby gate (ring barrier type). Dowels are sold at hardware stores, where they will usually cut them to the length you want. For medium to large dogs, dowels should be about six inches long and three-quarters of an inch wide or the same diameter as your dog's dumbbell. For little dogs, go with four to five inches long and as close to dumbbell diameter as available. Velcro is found at stores that sell sewing supplies.

In addition, you will need your lead, longe and fifty-foot light line.

TEACHING THE EXERCISE

This exercise is really two exercises that will be taught and practiced separately. Even after your dog is competing in Utility, it is smart to practice the two sections alone more often than together.

Since your dog is used to retrieving, the easiest way to teach the go-out is to pretend that it is just another type of retrieve.

Introducing the Dowels

Stick a Velcro square on two dowels about an inch from the end. With your dog on lead, place a dowel on the ground about three feet in front of her and have

Set up a miniature ring when your dog will do long line go-outs. Always send her to a barrier, and stick your dowels on it with Velcro whenever possible.

her retrieve it. Guide her to the dowel if she refuses, but don't repeat the fetch command. If she still balks at picking it up, ear pinch.

Practice retrieving dowels off the ground with much praise until she is accustomed to them and needs no corrections. Then make it fun by clicking the dowels together, moving around and teasing her with them before tossing one for her to retrieve. Don't do formal fronts.

Beginning the Go-Out

Find a wall or barrier you can use for practicing and stick the matching Velcro squares on it at about your dog's nose level. Place your dog on a sit-stay about three feet from the wall and enthusiastically ask, "Where's your dowels?" as she watches you stick them to the wall. Return to heel position and give your fetch command but add the word *go* in front of it ("Mancha, go fetch" or "Go take it"). When she brings back a dowel, make a happy fuss. If she doesn't, guide her to the dowel and ear pinch only if she still refuses. If she tries to bring both at once, reel her in gently as soon as she grabs the first dowel.

Work on this for two weeks, making sure your dog sees you place the dowel on the wall every time, and always ask, "Where's your dowels?" Use as many different walls and barriers in as many locations as possible. Set up your baby gate so that a push or pull won't knock it over and place dowels on it frequently, too.

Gradually move back until your dog is a six-foot lead length from the dowels and sometimes has slight tension on the lead as she goes out to retrieve.

Distance and Difficulty. After two weeks, place the dowels on the wall before you bring your dog over, so she doesn't see you place them. Then sit her at heel, three feet away, ask, "Where's your dowels?" and send her when she looks in the right direction. Gradually increase the distance to lead length and continue using as many different locations as you can. When your dog is reliable at lead length, use the longe, and when she performs at fifteen feet, set up a mini Utility ring so that she goes out to the dowels between the jumps. As you switch to your light line and slowly increase distance, expand your little ring proportionally. Eventually you want your dog to go out more than forty feet.

General Rules for Go-Outs

- Excite your dog every time by saying, "Where's your dowels?" Later that will cue her in the ring.
- If your dog starts to anticipate, keep some tension on the line (but don't jerk) and release the tension when you say, "Go."
- Always send your dog to a barrier of some type: wall, fence, hedge, gate.

244

- When sending your dog to a barrier that won't take the Velcro, prop your dowels up against it like a stickman.
- Move the go-out location after three go-outs. By varying the location, you teach your dog to go wherever you send her rather than marking or remembering a particular location.
- Since your dog thinks this exercise is a retrieve, correct with an ear pinch if she refuses to go out or doesn't make an effort to look for the dowels. When she is trying, but can't locate the dowels, guide her all the way to them and pinch only if she sees them and still won't take them.

Common Errors of the Dog and Simple Corrections

Veering off-center (arcing). Arcing is normal when using lines on go-outs, but you have to use them to keep your dog from taking a jump on the way out. Place a blockade of some sort (post, utility box) so that when your dog arcs to the side it keeps her a little closer to center. Gradually move the blockade closer to the middle of the ring as the go-outs become straighter. If your dog tries to go around the blockade, put tension on the line and only give slack when she tries to go on the correct side of the obstruction. ·

Heading for the corners (marking where the glove was). Generally, let your dog hunt until she finds the dowels, but don't use verbal encouragement because she should do it on her own. If you correct her too soon, she will lose confidence and be afraid to try. A dog who fears go-outs is harder to work with than one who simply marks the corners. Reducing the distance for several days and slowly extending it again may help.

Distractions and Proofing. Try to attach or lean dowels on any kind of barriers you haven't used yet (ropes, cement walls).

Work your dog where there is activity nearby, especially on the other side of the barrier. People playing with dogs, sitting on the ground, eating, running and clapping are all excellent distractions.

Prepare your dog for angled mats, lines in the ring that will have to be crossed (like tennis courts), fully matted rings and grass. Also practice with the jumps closer together and farther apart than normal.

Introducing the Turn and Sit

Remember random drops? Now it's random sits. When you are walking together casually (not heeling) and your dog isn't expecting a command, say her name and "Sit" in a firm but pleasant voice. She should turn to face you when she hears her name and sit immediately on the command. When teaching, step in toward her and pull upward on the lead rather gently the first several times to

Teaching the turn and sit. Command "Sit," snub up your lead and step in to prevent forward movement and to praise.

guide her into the sit. Later, if she fails to respond immediately, use the upward jerk sit correction.

Combining the Go-Out and Turn and Sit

When your dog can do fifteen-foot (or more) go-outs between the jumps in strange places on the first try and has been introduced to the turn and sit, she is ready to try them together.

With dowels on the wall and your dog on lead about five feet away, tell her to go out for her dowel. Just before she reaches for it, give your sit command. Stop her forward motion with steady pressure on the lead (don't jerk), walk in to encourage a quick sit and praise physically and verbally. When she no longer needs you to step in and sits with little tension on the lead, begin increasing the distance slowly. Try it off lead sometimes after she sits on command without lead tension. It will take time to go the full distance because it isn't good to practice the turn and sit in combination with the go-out very often.

General Rules for Practice

- For the first month, do only one turn and sit per lesson in combination with the go-out. It is okay to practice turn and sits randomly on lead though.
- Never command the turn and sit if your dog is doing a poor go-out. Instead, let her look for the dowels. If she quits or tries to take the jump, lead her to the dowels.
- When your dog is confident on go-outs and turn and sits, begin turning her 50 percent of the time on the first go-out in a new location, but let her retrieve the dowel on the second go-out. At a show your dog must think that even though she didn't get a dowel on the first go-out, there is one out there and she had better try for it the second time.
- As your dog becomes ring ready, only do about four go-outs per location (two for dowels and two for turn and sits), then switch locations. No matter how well trained your dog, never stop practicing with dowels.

Common Errors of the Dog and Simple Corrections

Arcing or button hooking before a sit or a slow sit. Practice random sits while your dog isn't training or expecting it and correct by running in and jerking upward.

Anticipating the turn and sit. Sometimes keep slight tension on the line as your dog goes out. If she fails to retrieve, ear pinch. Also fake her out by coughing or pretending to talk to someone as she goes out and be ready to enforce the retrieve.

Leave just enough distance between the jumps for you to stand. Signal the jump with one hand and hold the lead against your body with the other. This way you won't accidently signal with both hands toward opposite jumps.

Introducing the Jumps

Set the bar jump just below the height of your dog's elbow and introduce her to it by walking over it with her several times. Use her name and "bar" as your command. Then put her on a sit-stay on one side of the jump, go to the other side and command "Mancha, bar." Praise and repeat until she finds it easy.

The Directional Signal. Set both your jumps under elbow height and place them side by side, three feet apart. Sit your dog in line with the inside standard of one of the jumps and two feet behind it. Go to the other side, put your lead over the jump and stand at the jump line (between the jumps and even with them). Say your dog's name, signal the jump, say "Bar" if it is the bar jump and step toward it. If you signaled the high jump, give the same command you used in Open to designate that jump. Make your signal clear. Your arm should be straight out to the side, shoulder height, with your palm facing your dog.

Ideally, your dog jumped the indicated jump and you ran to meet her (so she doesn't have to turn to meet you yet) and praised her profusely. But maybe not. If she moved on her name, before you could give the directional signal, correct her back into a sit-stay and start over. If she tried to skip the jump or take the wrong one, use the lead to guide her over the correct one and next time walk toward the jump while praising. Keep your lead-holding hand close to your chest as your other hand signals; this will prevent you from accidentally giving two different signals.

Increasing the Angle and Distance of the Jumps. When your dog goes over the jump every time without trying to walk around it, begin inching her closer to the center line between the jumps. Increase the angle even farther by gradually moving her off-center toward the opposite jump. When she is reliable at an extreme angle, place her in the middle between the jumps and continue increasing the angle by gradually moving the jumps farther apart and your dog farther back from the jump line. Continue practicing with your dog off-center as well. You should still remain right at the jump line for ease of correction.

As your jumps get farther apart, stop flipping your lead over the jump, as your dog will soon associate that with the directional signal. If your jump standards are low enough, your lead will come over the top of them as you walk toward the jump. If not, drop your lead as your dog commits to the jump.

When your dog seems to be catching on to direction but still needs to see you move toward the jump, toss a toy on the other side of the jump for her to grab when she lands. Wait until she is obviously committed to jumping the correct jump before throwing it. If the toy makes her forget everything else, wait until she is in midair before throwing it.

To prevent anticipation, fake out your dog sometimes by saying her name, waiting a few seconds and then coughing or picking something off the ground instead of signaling. If she moves, correct her for breaking the sit-stay.

Once the toy has been introduced and your dog reliably takes direction and has been proofed against anticipation, remove your lead and begin raising the jumps two inches every five or six days. If your dog shows the slightest tendency to go under the bar jump, place a little circle of chicken wire under it.

Sometimes it will be obvious that your dog is focused on the wrong jump. In that case, say her name and cough or bend your knees, hoping she'll anticipate so that you can correct her back into a sit-stay and start over.

When your dog heads for the wrong jump, stop her by walking toward her while saying "Uh-uh." Don't try to cut her off at the pass or she will think you are running toward the jump because you want her to take it. When you get to her, signal toward the correct jump with one arm and lead her toward it with your other hand on her collar. When you are several feet from the jump, let her go so she can get her jumping rhythm, but continue signaling.

As your dog succeeds, keep spreading your jumps gradually and moving back from the jump line. Jumps will be around twenty feet apart at the show and you will stand twenty feet behind the jump line, but it is good to vary the distance during practice and often try for a greater angle and more distance.

Combining It All

The go-out, turn and sit and directed jumping come together as one exercise at the show, so your dog has to practice them in combination sometimes. Sometimes, but not always.

Use dowels at least 50 percent of the time on the go-out instead of adding the turn and sit. Walk out to your sitting dog sometimes to praise and release her. Occasionally signal the jumps. After a successful jump, often run backward so that your dog hurries to you and praise her physically and verbally when she catches you. Sometimes turn to face her when she is in midair, wait for her to come to front and command the finish. Soon facing her while standing still will cue your dog that she is expected to front. When she fronts, praise and release her some of the time, but occasionally add the finish.

Common Errors of the Dog and Simple Corrections

Missing the signal and/or not moving from the sit. Never give a second command. While still signaling, walk up to your dog, take her collar in your other hand and lead her partway to the jump.

IN THE RING

Responsibility of the Dog

- Sit at heel.
- Go out on command.

- Keep going until the handler gives the sit command, then turn and sit.
- Watch the handler for jump direction.
- Jump the correct jump.
- Front and finish.

Responsibility of the Handler

- Talk to your dog as you line up for the go-out. Use the cue words ("Where's your dowels?") you always use at practice to let her know that a go-out is next.
- Stop your dog's go-out intelligently. If she is going nice and straight, let her get way out before stopping her. If she is veering hard, seems confused or looks as if she might stop on her own, give the sit command as soon as you are sure she went beyond the ten feet necessary to pass.
- Think before you signal the jumps. They may both look "high," but one is called the "bar."
- Make your commands clear and your directional signals deliberate.
- Stand straight. Don't lean into your signals or hold them excessively.
- Pivot toward your dog while she is in midair.
- Keep your hands at your sides after signaling.

Common Handler Errors and Simple Corrections

Flashing directional signals too fast.
Using excessive body English.

Passing

Your dog should pass if she waits for your command to leave and then goes out between the jumps and ten or more feet past them. She must then stop and wait for your directional signal, jump the hurdle you send her to and return within your easy reach. She must do the exercise twice and may not jump a hurdle on the way out or knock over either jump.

When your dog tries to take the wrong jump, correct her by saying "Uh-uh" as you walk up to her collar. Then keep signaling as you start her toward the correct jump.

Show Business: Utility

Review "Show Business: Open" (see page 191).

Before You Enter

- Review "Show Business: Open" (see page 191).
- Practice with rings of various sizes and shapes. You may also encounter rings with lines on the ground or oddly located posts.
- Tasks are more complex in Utility, so things you may not even notice can cause even well-trained dogs to fail. Since Utility teaches your dog to become more aware of subtle signals, such as varying where you hold your hand (at your waist versus at your side), saying her name before a command when she isn't used to it or releasing her between exercises if you don't at home can cause tremendous confusion. Note which procedures you normally follow and either be consistent or practice inconsistency.

At the Show

- Give the steward your jump heights when you pick up your armband.
- One or two dogs before your turn, give the steward your articles and gloves.

When It's Your Turn

- You can talk to your dog while lining up for the exercises and respond with "Ready" before the start of any exercises, including the signals. (Use "Yes" before the go-out.)

UTILITY:
Turning It Blue

Signal Exercise

IF YOU'VE BEEN WORKING to turn it blue, you already know how important good heeling, fronts, finishes and especially attention are to a winning performance. You have better odds of winning the lottery than of earning good scores on the signal exercise if you can't elicit absolute attention around any distraction. To obtain and maintain that attention review the sections on distractions in "An Ounce of Prevention" (see page 111). Use distractions like someone unfolding a chair and sitting next to your dog, a door opening from behind her, someone bouncing popcorn off her back and loud clapping. If you don't normally train with people who can help you distract, tape-record noises like guests arriving or preparing dog food.

EYES IN THE BACK OF HER HEAD

Use fake outs to call the bluff of clever dogs who sneak a peek elsewhere and assume that you've given a signal as they catch movement out of the corner of their eye. When your dog glances away, dip your shoulder or bend your knees. If she moves out of position, correct as described in the "Earning the Green" text for this exercise. But if she just flinches and catches herself, give praise.

Reward intense stares by occasionally releasing your dog and throwing out a ball when she is expecting a signal. Your dog is more likely to give that intense stare if you never do more than three to five signals at a time before either releasing, returning or completing the sequence.

If slow drops are your concern, use distractions to try to make your dog forget her work so that you can correct for total disobedience. If she practices signal exercise drops on uncomfortable surfaces, your dog won't be prissy in the ring.

The speed at which you correct can make or break the effectiveness of a correction. Walk in to correct a confused, anticipating or beginning dog. Run in to correct a dog who is distracted or just blanks you out.

STANDING AT ATTENTION

Your dog should be attentive as you stand her so she will end up in heel position. Also, if she is inattentive right at your side it will take considerable optimism to believe she will focus on you when you signal from across the ring. If your dog still forges on the stand, do a "Jackie Gleason left turn" as soon as her shoulder is in a slightly forged position, even if you have already started to signal. Some dogs have a tendency to want to sit on the stand signal after that correction, so be prepared to touch her stifle after you signal as a reminder.

Make it easier for your attentive dog to stop in heel position by coordinating your stand signal with your footwork. You need to stop at the completion of your signal.

OVERCOMING DIFFICULTIES

The signal exercise is unique in that even dogs who do it well in all sorts of test situations can still blow it in the ring. Make this evasive exercise less challenging by using every quirky distraction you can think of. Vary each attempt with fake outs, returning to praise, releasing, giving the signals at different time intervals and not making your dog do a long series of signals.

Scent Discrimination

ENTHUSIASTIC PRAISE after smart turns will not only improve the sharpness of the sit but will also prevent anticipating going out to the pile. Correct crooked sits and errors during the turn as you would if they occurred during heeling.

GIVING SCENT

Folks assume that you allow your dog to smell your hand so that she knows what scent to look for. But if your dog has lived with you long enough for you to train her through Utility, she already knows every nuance of your scent. So giving scent is actually a signal that you are doing articles and she should pay attention. If your dog looks away as you flash your right hand three inches from her nose, quickly give the ''around'' command and jump ahead if she lags on the turn. Before long she will pay attention and prepare for the turn when you give scent.

WHERE HAVE MY ARTICLES GONE?

Judges may put the pile of articles in every imaginable place in the ring: in front of the gate or jumps, alongside ring barriers, between jumps and parallel to them. Changing the location of your articles every training session will teach your dog that "Find it" means the pile is straight ahead after the turn. Training in grass tall enough to obscure the articles from view will bring the point home and is absolutely necessary if you plan to show a small dog outdoors. Practice on line so you can snub up if she detours.

RING-READY PROOFING

After your dog has been working the full set of articles for a month, practice having your articles scented and placed by a variety of people in a variety of places. Offer your helpers some "finger food" first, to proof against donut-eating stewards.

Sometimes a dog will step on an article and turn it on end or kick it out of the pile. Proof by sometimes placing an article cockeyed during practice.

Arrange your articles imaginatively, using circles, squares, Xs and random placement. Judges do.

Place your scented article in various places in the pile to encourage your dog to move around the articles looking for the scent. If one position is hardest for her, place the article there often.

Practice on tall or wet grass, on plush, relatively short ground covers and next to moving dogs, children and handlers. Be creative by practicing in a chicken coop or horse stall. Many shows called "indoor" are actually held inside animal barns at fairgrounds, and the floors are made of dirt plus. At one show a dog was told to "Find it" and happily brought back a dried cow pie. The unamused judge instructed the handler to "Take it."

Keep you cool during the teaching phase of this exercise, and your dog will eventually learn to work the articles steadily and reliably. Then your only challenge is perfecting the turn and the usual fronts and finishes.

Directed Retrieve

SLOPPY RETRIEVING HABITS cause major point losses. Practice throwing your glove out a short distance and sending your dog to fetch. Don't make it formal. You want her in the frolicking mood that made her flub the glove at the show. If your dog tosses or mouths the glove, give her a jerk and hope that she drops it—then you can give an ear pinch correction. If she only fools around with the glove when she is off lead, practice throwing the glove close and be ready to run in and rap her under the jaw, then jerk as you back up and praise.

Don't rip the glove out of your dog's mouth. Command "Give," and expect her to release it. If she doesn't, tap her underjaw firmly enough to startle her, and praise her for releasing.

PERFECTING THE TURN

There are several things you can do to help your dog perfect her turn:

- *Use head cues.* Begin looking in the direction of the turn as you give your command. When she sees this head motion, she will know exactly where to go when you move.
- *Use consistent footwork.* Moving your right foot first to indicate your direction, then your left foot to give your dog something to line up with

Look in the direction of your turn just before moving.

works well. End by squaring up with your right foot to give your dog time to turn and sit well.

- *Praise lavishly after 50 percent of your turns.* Attention and precision will improve as your dog concentrates on earning that praise. But when she goofs off, correct errors as if they had occurred during heeling.

DIRECTION-PROOFING TRICKS

Introduce tricks a lead length away and gradually work up to longe line and finally twenty-five foot light line distances. Using tricks will challenge your dog's direction-taking abilities and make the glove exercise—even at outdoor shows with uneven terrain and long grass—seem easy. Insist that your dog watch you to receive the signal after the glove turn. Correct inattention with a jerk and an "Uh-uh" or a sneakaway.

Staggered gloves: Place the glove you will send your dog to 30 percent farther away than it will be in the ring. Put the other gloves in their normal positions.

Hidden gloves: When you originally taught your dog this exercise, you sent her to a hidden glove a lead length away. Now place the other gloves in sight and send her for a hidden one.

Tossed Glove: Place two gloves in sight. Turn your dog to one of them, then throw out the missing glove. For instance, if you are sending her to glove number 3, place gloves in positions 1 and 3. After turning your dog to face glove 3, throw a glove into the number 2 spot. Then signal and send your dog to 3.

Angles Afar: Position yourself in the normal spot, then, if your dog is on lead, take one large step forward before turning and sending. If your dog is on the longe, take three large steps forward; take five steps if you are using the twenty-five-foot cord.

Once dogs take direction, turn smoothly and learn that the glove must be retrieved like a dumbbell, not "killed" like a Raggedy Ann doll, near-perfect scores should become commonplace.

The Norfolk Terrier, Ch. Tylwyth Just Chelsea, Am., Can. UD, CG, owned by Mary D. Fine, boasts a fine record of wins in the breed ring and accomplishments in the most demanding area of Utility obedience. The initials C.G. stand for certificate of gameness and indicate that this dog can do the Terrier's traditional work. *Janet Ashbey*

Moving Stand and Examination

PERFECTING THE FINE POINTS

ALTHOUGH THE MOVING STAND is probably the easiest Utility exercise to train a dog to pass, earning a perfect score on it can be difficult.

The following are some common problems of the moving stand.

Arcing when coming into heel. You already learned the benefits of using props to limit your dog's options and get her patterned into a routine. They work well here, too. Put your dog on line and position her so that she will run into a pole unless she comes in straight. If no pole or tree is handy, use chicken wire or some other object. Snub up the line if she attempts to go on the wrong side of the object and use the prop consistently for at least two months.

Slowness. Unlike most exercises where speed improves as you get farther away, many dogs become more tentative the farther they have to come because they have more time to worry whether they should be doing a front or a call to heel. Alleviate some of the confusion by changing your foot position. If you keep your feet together on the front, have them shoulder width apart on the moving stand or vice versa.

Poor sits. Correct such errors the same as you would any finish.

Anticipating the stand or call. Fake out your dog by bending your knees as you say "Stand your dog" and continue walking. After being instructed to call your dog to heel during practice run-throughs, always wait two seconds or slightly more before responding.

INCREASING CONFIDENCE AND SPEED

Instead of facing your dog directly, turn slightly to the right during the early stages of practice. Heel position will be a little closer, and she may feel less intimidated than when she has to come head on into you before going to heel. Gradually straighten your position as she becomes secure.

Say "Ready, ya ready!" before calling your dog in. Stand six feet away on lead and only occasionally go farther away off lead.

Throw a ball out behind you as your dog passes your left leg to go to heel.

Give food or play with a ball after your dog comes into sitting position at heel. Don't let her know you have anything before giving her the reward—otherwise it becomes a bribe.

The more you try to entice your dog into moving fast with running and coaxing, the worse speed problems can become. Instead, try familiarizing her with the pattern. As confidence increases, speed often does too.

Directed Jumping

$\mathbf{I}$F YOU don't already have a set of portable jumps and ring barriers, this exercise will convince you that those training tools are no longer a luxury—they are a necessity.

PERFECTING THE FINE POINTS

Teaching directed jumping may test your dedication, because training in unfamiliar places is essential.

Go-Outs

Dogs quickly memorize training areas where they have done go-outs, so train in a totally new location at least twice a week. Send your dog to different barriers; walls, fences, hedges, ring ropes and baby gates. Vary sending her to the middle of the gate as well as the stanchions, and always use ring barriers at least as long as the side of a ring.

Place distractions your dog may want to avoid on the other side of the barrier close to where she will have to sit. If she fears huge, hairy dogs, find some Old English Sheepdogs or a couple of Newfs and ask their owners to stand close to the barrier with them. If your dog loves kids, particularly the popcorn-eating variety, place some in the corner with a load of munchies and correct your dog if she is drawn their way.

Cue your dog by asking, "Where's your dowels?" both in practice and at shows. In the ring, when the judge asks if you are ready, respond "Yes." Since your dog knows "ready" means to watch you, avoid taking her concentration from the dowels by saying that before the go-out.

Corner Go-Outs

Practice frequently with side barriers because many dogs are drawn to corners. Even if the side barriers only extend a few feet from the back barrier, your training area will appear more ringlike.

After your dog has been going out for her dowels for about two months and is even hard to distract in new locations, have her do the glove exercise to one of the corner gloves before the go-out. Then place a highly visible glove near each jump and send her out for her dowels as usual. Stop her with tension on the line if she goes to the glove, and guide her to the dowel if she doesn't make the effort to find it herself. As she learns to ignore the gloves, gradually move them toward the corners.

The Turn and Sit

The straightness of the sit is not scored, but promptness is. Creeping forward is also points off. Once dogs practice jumping after the sit, many automatically sit facing you in anticipation of the signal. If your dog sits turned toward one jump at practice, send her to the opposite one rather than correcting her sit.

Proof your dog against anticipating the sit and stopping short by coughing as she is going out. If she interprets that as an excuse to stop, ear pinch while leading her to the dowel.

Creeping, sniffing and not turning promptly are best corrected separately from the go-out. Do random turn and sits in nontraining situations when your dog least expects it. Correct creeping by swinging her back into place and jerking upward, just as you would for a broken sit-stay. Stop sniffing by rapping under the jaw. Speed up sits by giving an upward jerk. Running in to correct will make a stronger impression on your dog than walking. Return and praise frequently to encourage a prompt sit and attention before jumping.

PROOFING THE JUMPS

Gradually separate your jumps up to forty feet apart (about double the ring distance). When that becomes easy, increase the angle. Sometimes place your dog only ten feet away from the jump line. Other times sit her in front of one jump and send her to the far one. Signal her to the close jump only 25 percent of the time. By varying the send you teach her to take direction rather than always expect to jump the far hurdle.

Rings with posts in them can disorient dogs. They seem to think that if they just go around what appears to be a jump standard, their job is done. Even if you never have to show in a ring with posts, practicing with one will improve your dog's comprehension of the exercise.

To teach your dog to be able to rethink her intentions when she appears mesmerized by one jump in the ring, walk her toward one jump, then stop and send her to the other.

Experiment with how far you need to turn as your dog jumps, to get her to come into a straight sit.

HANDLING

Turn and sit your dog just before she reaches the ring barrier to avoid a deduction for sniffing it. An exception is if the ring is unusually long. Then turn your dog about twenty feet beyond the line of the jumps.

The Brittany, Ch. Three B's Rae of Sunshine, CD, owned, trained and handled by Sheryl Rilea and bred by Bob and Mona Proctor.   *Stephen Klein*

Fast Work

$\mathbf{F}$AST WORK will help your dog respond to commands without needing a warm-up. It may also improve her attitude and make you a more competent trainer. Fun and quick, fast work make for an enjoyable training session. It should be made up of exercises your dog already knows, not ones she is just learning. Do as much or as little as you like by filling an entire training session with it or using it as a change of pace.

Begin by writing a list of exercises or parts of exercises. A Novice list might look like this: thirty seconds of heeling (concentrating on change of pace), front, stand, recall, lineup, front, off-lead heeling (concentrating on about turns and halts), front, figure eight, fifteen seconds of play, finish, etc.

Arrange your equipment (lines, jumps, retrieving objects) before you begin. Move from exercise to exercise quickly, but don't coax. Tell your dog, "Ready, ya ready, let's go" and run to the starting point. If your dog doesn't follow briskly, stop, take her collar and correct with a jerk as you accelerate. Always insist on a straight lineup, but quickly straighten her by taking her collar, rather than waiting for her to fidget into the proper position. Never repeat an exercise. If she does it wrong, correct her but wait for it to come up on the list again to see if she can do it correctly cold.

Ten minutes of fast work can accomplish a great deal. But if you aren't sweating when you are done, either you've been training for the Olympics or you didn't work hard enough. Line up sharply, use lots of verbal enthusiasm and keep moving as much as possible.

Here are some exercises, their components and a few proofing techniques to include in your list of fast work, depending on how advanced your dog is. Use some fake outs to prevent anticipation and list difficult exercises several times, but never in a row. It is easiest to have a helper read the list as you work, but you can tape it to a tree or the wall if it is too difficult to memorize.

Heeling, on and off lead

change of pace: fast, slow, transition into and out of
turns: right, left, abouts, left Us
heeling into walls
figure eight
pinpointing: reverse, tuck, ready, lineups

Stand

heel into a stand
stand from a sit
examination
return and praise before release
stand for measurement

Recalls

fronts
angles
with front box
drop a toy from your chin or food from your mouth
"thinner thighs in thirty recalls" position

Finish

against walls

Drop on recall

random drops
call, drop, then release from a distance or return

Retrieve

hidden (in cover)
placed
near jump
thrown long distance
on end
broken dumbbell
under gate, table or chair

Retrieve over jump

retrieve over bar jump
angles

Broad jump

throw toy or run when dog is in midair
front box to practice turn and front

Signals

heel, stand, stay, down, sit, recall, finish
release if dog is watching intently
on different surfaces

Scent articles

turn
article slightly out of pile
articles placed in different patterns (X, T, straight line)

Directed retrieve (gloves)

turns
staggered
thrown
extreme angles
hidden or camouflaged glove

Moving stand

stand without hesitation during heeling
examine thoroughly
call to heel

Directed jumping

go-out
random sits
jumps
    off-center
    ten feet from jump line
    forty feet from jump line
    obstacles in the middle
    walking toward one jump and sending toward the other

Dogs are for loving

Dogs Are for Loving

No MATTER how deeply involved in the dog game we are by now, the reason we acquired our first dog is as valid today as it was then. Dogs are for companionship. Before we ever thought of becoming exhibitors, we made dogs part of our lives simply because we loved them.

A dual-ring dog is a double delight. Because her body and her brains have both been developed, she is pleasing to the eye and a pleasure to live with. But whenever the show ring is involved, there will be times of frustration as well as days of elation. During the down days it may help to remember that before ribbons, before ratings and before show rings, there was still the special relationship between dog and man. A good training program enhances that relationship, but frustration causes some trainers to tear it down—and that is a pity for both partners. There is always another dog show, but relationships are special.

Glossary

Arcing. Not following a straight path to the destination.

Break off. Release and play.

Bumping and crowding. When the dog's head or body touches the handler.

CD—Companion Dog. American Kennel Club title earned by dogs who have acquired three qualifying scores in Novice obedience at dog shows or obedience trials.

CDX—Companion Dog Excellent. American Kennel Club title earned by dogs who have acquired three qualifying scores in Open obedience at dog shows or obedience trials.

Curly Q. Circling tightly to the right after completing the arc around the right post of the figure eight. Used to teach the dog to wrap when heeling around the right post.

Curving. *See* Arcing.

Distractions. Any outside influence that attracts the dog's attention and makes her perform poorly.

Fake Out. Making a motion or sound when the dog is expecting a command. Used to proof against anticipation.

Forging. When the dog's shoulder is ahead of the handler's.

Guiding. Making the dog complete the exercise correctly by taking the lead or collar and silently forcing as firmly as necessary.

Head cues. Indicating speed or direction changes by moving your head.

Jackie Gleason left turn. Pivoting 90 degrees to the left on the right foot and swinging the left leg slightly back and then forward toward the dog so that your left foot passes under her front feet. Used during heeling and on turns in place to stop forging and crowding by medium and large dogs.

Jerk. Snapping and releasing the dog to correct. Done in different directions (up, down and to the side), depending on the problem to be corrected. Not intended to physically move the dog, but rather to prompt her into a previously trained response.

Jumping into the lead. A type of lead correction. Used to correct lagging, sniffing, wideness and inattention by pushing off the ball of your right foot so that you can leap forward with your left, causing the lead to tighten. When used following right and about-turns, step in the new direction with the right foot so that you can leap with your left on the second step.

Jump line. An imaginary line running straight across from one jump to another.

Lagging. When the dog's nose falls behind the handler's shoulder.

Light line. Fifty-foot line made of venetian blind cord or nylon twine, used as a bridging step to off-lead control.

Line up. Assuming heel position at a predetermined point to begin an exercise.

Longe line. Fifteen-foot nylon line used on sneakaways and intermediate stays, recalls, retrieves and jumps.

Marking corners. Tendency for dogs who retrieve the number 1 or number 3 glove to go to that area when sent on the go-out.

Motivation. Interacting with your dog to encourage movement, playing and a happy attitude.

Mouthing the dumbbell. Biting or shifting the dowel around in the mouth.

No pulling rule. Teaching your dog to walk next to you on a loose lead.

Off-lead correction. Using the tab to correct rather than touching the line.

OTCh.—Obedience Trial Champion. American Kennel Club title won by UD dogs who have accumulated 100 points. It is the only obedience title earned by defeating other dogs.

Release. Freeing the dog from a command with a consistently used word.

Reel in. Pulling the dog to you smoothly, hand over hand, without jerking.

Set up. Recreating events that may induce your dog to make a mistake that you are prepared to correct.

Sky hooks. Fishing sinkers strung together with monofilament. Used for solving runaway problems.

Slack. Having no tension in a lead.

Sneakaways. Technique used to get attention, stop pulling, teach respect and prepare the dog for heeling.

Snub up. Tightening the line without jerking it to prevent the dog from moving any farther in the wrong direction.

Taut. Having a little tension in a lead.

UD—Utility Dog. American Kennel Club title earned by dogs who have acquired three qualifying scores in Utility obedience at dog shows or obedience trials.

Wideness. When the dog is not as close as possible without touching the handler.